BANK FISHING FOR RESERVOIR TROUT

An Introduction

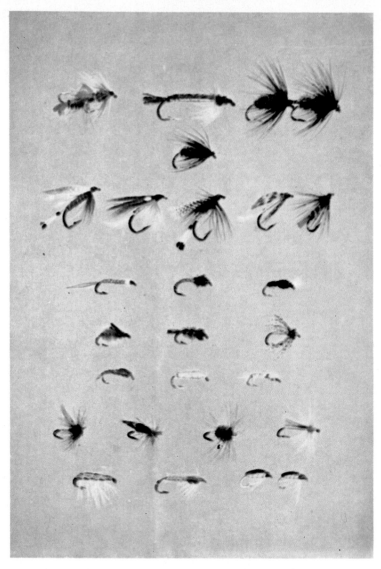

A SELECTION OF FLIES DESCRIBED IN CHAPTER 6

Lures
Worm Fly   Jersey Herd   Black & Peacock Tandem

Wet Flies
Black & Peacock Spider
Mallard & Claret   Dunkeld   Peter Ross   Silver Invicta   Zulu

Buzzer Patterns
Red Larva   Footballer   Black Buzzer

Nymphs
Brown   Green & Brown   Green
Pheasant Tail   Grayling Lure   Grey Goose

Dry Flies
Black Gnat   Sedge   Coch-y-Bonddu   Midge

Stand-bys
Shrimper   Sedge Pupa   Corixa

Jim Calver

Bank Fishing
for
Reservoir Trout

AN INTRODUCTION

Adam & Charles Black
London

FIRST PUBLISHED 1972
SECOND EDITION 1979
A. & C. BLACK (PUBLISHERS) LTD
35 BEDFORD ROW, LONDON WC1R 4JH

© 1972 & 1979 JAMES B. CALVER

ISBN: 0 7136 1881 7

DEDICATION
To Dee, for all her love

Printed in Great Britain by
REDWOOD BURN LIMITED
Trowbridge & Esher

Contents

Photographs

Figures

Introduction

At the time of starting this book I had just completed my first ten seasons of bank fishing for reservoir trout. I started as a beginner and feel I have acquired a little experience and knowledge which may help other beginners to enjoy this sport as much as I do.

My first interests in fishing of any kind were started in about 1955 at which time my elder son David, then about ten years old, was becoming quite proficient at coarse fishing. His enthusiasm infected me and he was my first instructor. We had many happy times fishing a stretch of the River Medway between Leigh and Penshurst—a few miles from our home at Sevenoaks, Kent, and I gradually learnt the art of catching roach, rudd, perch, chub and dace and thoroughly enjoyed it. I made friends with other fishermen and during 1959 reports were coming through of a new type of fishing which was available at the recently constructed reservoir named Weir Wood, near Forest Row in Sussex, some twenty-five miles from our home. It seemed from all accounts that good trout were there to be caught and news of this kind is something of a rarity in south-east England, where any form of trout fishing is very hard to find.

In late summer 1959 I went over to Weir Wood after reading a booklet published by the North-West Sussex Water Board covering the rules and facilities for trout fishing in their new reservoir. These rules made it quite clear that 'traditional fly fishing methods' were the only ones permitted, and despite my complete ignorance of fly fishing as a whole I looked forward to finding out what it was all about.

The term 'reservoir' intrigued me as I had visions of some huge concrete-faced tank or vast water enclosure which might remain as a permanent blemish to the Sussex countryside. I was astonished to find how this new, artificial lake blended so naturally into the surrounding farm land and wooded outskirts of Ashdown Forest.

After a most friendly chat with the bailiff, it was soon perfectly clear that, if I wanted to try my hand at catching trout from this or any other similar reservoir, I would need to learn a totally different form of fishing from that which I had practised on the River Medway during my limited experience to date. I had not the slightest knowledge of fly fishing, neither had I any fly fishing tackle. I was most anxious to learn but where should I begin? Looking back to that stage and my subsequent search for suitable reading and instruction, I know I would have found a book in simple language for beginners most useful.

The aim of this book is to fill that gap and provide the beginner with advice which I hope will lead him (or her) to enjoy and succeed in fly fishing for trout from the banks of reservoirs, lakes or other still water fisheries.

In this revised edition I have avoided too much technical detail, as there are some excellent books available for more detailed study, written by highly skilled and very experienced reservoir fishermen. I refer to parts of these books in the various chapters and Appendix B includes a summary of the books which I have found most helpful up to the present time and suggestions for further reading.

I wish to thank everyone who has helped me to prepare this book. First to the expert fishermen—authors T. C. Ivens and John Goddard for their kind permission to include photographs from *Still Water Fly Fishing* and *Trout Flies of Still Water* respectively, and to Frank Sawyer for permission to quote from a letter advising on suitable methods for fishing the leaded nymphs which he has devised, and then to Dr Digby Lewis for the drawings of aquatic fly life originally included in his article 'The Trout's Larder' published in the June 1970 edition of *Trout and Salmon*; to Mr G. M. Swales, retired Manager of the East Surrey Water Company for permission to include photographs of Bough Beech Reservoir; to David Wallis for his enthusiasm, skill and patience in all aspects of his photographic work; to Les Sawyer, Bailiff at Bough Beech Reservoir for his good-humoured, forthright comments and advice upon parts of the text; to my dear friends in Somerset, John and Margot Burgess without whose experience and instruction I would never have learnt the style of bank fishing which I most enjoy; to Barry Grafton, who started reservoir bank fishing in 1970 and provided me with a comprehensive summary of all he hoped to find included in a 'Beginner's Book' and for his practical help with the knot-tying experiments and general proof-checking; to the cheerful bailiffs on all reservoirs without whose long working hours and supervision this sport could not exist; to all my fishing friends and to other anglers I know by sight, each of whom during the course of conversation has passed on useful information;

As I have no business connections with any tackle manufacturers or suppliers I feel free to recommend certain items bearing proprietary names in the hope that the beginner may be guided towards getting well tried basic tackle at reasonable cost.

Since the first edition of this book there have been two major developments which are relevant to this sport. Firstly, the research and development of rich feeding at some trout farms have led to several species of monster trout which are produced mainly for breeding purposes. Some of the smaller privately owned lakes and fisheries include some very large fish as part of special stocking but when writing generally for the beginner I am assuming he or she will spend the greater part of their time on day ticket reservoirs where the general run of trout caught are between about 1 lb and 4 lb— with the occasional big ones of perhaps 6–8 lb or so and my recommendations for both tactics and tackle are geared accordingly.

Secondly, the arrival of carbon-fibre (sometimes referred to as graphite) as the newest rod building material has led to a whole new range of excellent fishing rods. Without doubt a carbon-fibre rod is both exceptionally light in weight and powerful in action but they are very expensive. The use of a carbon-fibre rod will not suddenly turn a bad caster into a good one neither will it enable a beginner to cast a neat line overnight. It is for this reason I do not recommend the beginner to incur the expense of a carbon-fibre rod at the outset of his fishing career.

To end this introduction, I would like to recommend bank fishing for reservoir trout as a thoroughly enjoyable form of relaxation because quite apart from the sport of catching a good edible fish there are endless opportunities for studying all forms of wild life at the waterside. If you are patient and observant you can gradually build up an elementary knowledge of entomology which will form a valuable background for your fishing tactics under the different conditions which arise during the course of a season and there will be a gradual accumulation of knowledge which will lead you to success.

JIM CALVER
Sevenoaks, Kent, 1979

1

Reservoirs and Opportunities for Trout Fishing

We live in a small country surrounded by sea and where it rains on and off for about nine months of the year, but if we are lucky enough to have several weeks of warm dry weather there are usually some regional warnings of a water shortage. In order to meet the need for a public water supply and to cater for redevelopment of our housing and industrial requirements throughout the land there must be facilities for the collection and storage of fresh water, and it is for this purpose that new reservoirs come into being. Any proposals for the acquisition of land for reservoir construction or other major development must always result in lengthy negotiations and public inquiries, and this is as it should be, because parts of our small island are of such outstanding beauty that if they are to be changed and sacrificed to meet our needs then the most careful and detailed consideration must be given to ensure that when development is complete it will blend as naturally as possible with the neighbouring landscape. Sites for open reservoir construction must be such that the subsoil is sufficiently impervious to retain a huge volume of water, and a few notes in layman's terms upon an imaginary new project of this kind are relevant to the subject of this book. Let's assume that after completion of all planning procedure a site for the construction of a new reservoir is finally confirmed and that a Water Company or Board is to be responsible for its construction and future management. In this imaginary project the stage is eventually reached where all claims for compensation are discharged to the satisfaction of all who

13

suffer loss. Such an ideal conclusion is best related to fiction because
in fact there are bound to be some most unfortunate cases of hard-
ship caused by loss of land, amenity or even livelihood which are
incapable of compensation in terms of money alone. In this project
a site of about four hundred acres of arable farm land with a valley
profile has been selected and the new reservoir is to be formed by
constructing a dam across the width of the valley and flooding about
two hundred and fifty acres back from the dam face. The design is
such that when the flooding reaches high water level the maximum
depth at the dam will be about seventy feet. In due course preliminary
work is started involving alterations to ditches, culverts and streams,
the demolition of any buildings which have been acquired and a most
careful scrutiny to ensure that any possible source of pollution is
eliminated. Old ponds must be emptied, trees felled and the site
excavated to the designed profile. Special consideration must be given
to ensure that water supplies are preserved for the maintenance and
daily needs of neighbouring farmland. The construction of the dam
may include a control tower and the general design will provide for
the overflow and disposal of surplus water. It follows that a reservoir
of this type, formed by damming and flooding a valley, will have
differing depths of water throughout its area and in general the water
will be very shallow at the margins with an increase in depth towards
the centre of the original valley. Another type of reservoir is formed
by excavation from relatively hilly ground and in this case it is probable that there will be areas of considerable depth right up to the
sloping margins. The sources of water supply for a new reservoir
vary considerably but in our imaginary case the main supply is to be
abstracted and piped from a nearby river and in addition several
underground streams are to be utilized as well. Further flooding will
occur by natural rainfall—some directly from the sky above and
some indirectly by ditches, culverts and feeder streams from the
Board's catchment area. Flooding up to the designed high water level
may take two or three years and during this period all kinds of building and engineering works will be in hand outside the flooded area
but within the site which was acquired for the complete project.
These works may include the construction of purification and pump-
ing stations, housing for resident staff and other buildings required
for the water engineering services as a whole. Roads, car parks and
extensive boundary fencing must be completed and above all the

design includes some careful landscaping and restoration work around the perimeter of the reservoir—including seeding or turfing disturbed ground as well as planting trees and shrubs so that the completed development blends as naturally as possible into the adjoining countryside.

Once a site for a new reservoir has been confirmed there are usually some fairly early approaches to the Board or other authority responsible for management of the project to see what kinds of recreational facilities will be available when the development is complete. These will come from various sectors of the public and will invariably be made by those interested in fishing, sailing, bird watching and the preservation of wild life. There will be others who would like access for general relaxation amongst the new scenery and requests from photographic enthusiasts as well. The facilities which can be offered will depend mainly upon the size and shape of the reservoir and the attitude of those responsible for its management. In an enormous complex the size of Grafham in Northamptonshire, extending to some sixteen hundred acres, it seems possible to cater for all who wish to come, and at Chew Valley Lake in Somerset there is a large enough area of water to support both fishing and sailing at the same time. In our imaginary reservoir with a water area of about two hundred and fifty acres there is insufficient room to accommodate both fishing and sailing during the same months, and the next chapter explains why. So in this case the Board decides to preserve an area of some fifty acres as a permanent bird sanctuary and nature reserve, the remainder to be available as a trout fishery from the first of May until the last day of September, after which date autumn and winter sailing facilities will be available until the beginning of the following fishing season. Unfortunately the Board cannot permit entry at random for others who wish to wander around, but they lay out a very attractive setting as a public viewing area with facilities for car parking and general relaxation. Such a point is that provided for public enjoyment at Clatworthy reservoir, high up in the Brendon Hills of Somerset and a very good example of this kind, where visitors from all parts are welcomed and enjoy the fine views extending across the reservoir. These preliminary notes on the formation of a new reservoir lead us into the subject of this book and now that the Board has agreed to form a trout fishery and permit autumn and winter sailing plus the formation of a bird sanctuary and a general amenity area as well, let's stretch our imagination to the utmost and assume that those interested in the respective facilities are generally satisfied with the arrangements.

At the present time there are several major reservoir projects under consideration, and it seems that in each case the provision of recreational facilities and the preservation of wild life are receiving the most detailed consideration. The Southern Water Authority has just completed and opened Bewl Bridge reservoir, the site of which lies on the Kent and Sussex county boundary. In this case a total area of about eleven hundred acres has been acquired, of which some seven hundred and seventy have been flooded. The reservoir is founded on the Wadhurst clays which form a watertight basin in the valley of the site. The Authority is carefully watching the effect on visual amenities of the area in which the reservoir has been constructed, and with its setting in an attractive wooded countryside there are opportunities for fishing and sailing as well as providing a series of waterside country walks and the creation of a wild life sanctuary. Fishing returns to date are very encouraging.

Farther north there are recently completed facilities for trout fishing at giant Rutland water which extends to some three thousand acres of fishery and this complex includes a nature reserve and sailing facilities plus extensive trout hatcheries under the skilled supervision of highly qualified staff. It will be interesting to see how these new waters compare with the older established reservoirs because it takes several years before a newly constructed reservoir can be assessed as a successful trout fishery or otherwise.

Fishing opportunities

From the time when a first cut is made into the site for a new reservoir there are factors which will affect its fishing potential. Due to the original valley profile in our imaginary case there will be marginal areas of very little depth, and as the sun warms up these shallows will harbour all kinds of valuable weed and nature will provide the aquatic insects to add to the rich worms, grubs and bottom feed which will be available in the newly-flooded arable land. The abundance of feed will support and encourage a rapid rate of growth in the trout which are to be brought from fish farms in other parts of the country to stock the reservoir. During hot summer months the deeper water will attract the trout into cooler surround-

Photograph 1. The western shore line of Bough Beech reservoir. A good example of a new reservoir blending into adjoining countryside by careful design and landscape restoration.

Photograph 2. A quiet and shallow bay in which large trout feed regularly in the marginal weed beds. The bank fisherman must preserve such valuable feeding grounds by avoiding clumsy wading and careless casting.

Above: Photograph 3. Part of a reservoir is usually preserved as a bird sanctuary where fishing and sailing are prohibited. Many species of fine birds settle into their new surroundings in a very short time.

Below: Photograph 4. The northern boundary of Bough Beech reservoir at Winkhurst Green. The photographs on this and the preceding page show parts of this reservoir, which was formed by damming and flooding an arable valley beneath Ide Hill, Kent and was first opened as a trout fishery in May 1970.

ings and there will be a number of small bays and sections of gravelly shore line holding a variety of small creatures which we shall study in more detail when considering the reservoir trout's feeding habits. Once a new reservoir attains a reasonable depth of flooding and before opening as a fishery it is usual to introduce trout on an experimental basis and arrange periodic catches so that rate of growth and general progress may be recorded and related to other factors which will formulate a stocking programme for the completed reservoir. Whether the reservoir is made by flooding arable land or a rocky site the areas of deeps and shallows will vary considerably and these physical factors will affect both fish and fishing methods. Fishing methods will dictate the type of tackle required and these aspects are dealt with from the beginner's standpoint in the following chapters. There are two principal methods of fishing for reservoir trout. The first is from the banks or by wading from them and the second by fishing from a boat. The title of this book makes clear the method we are going to study.

Whether you fish from the bank or boat physical fitness is required and I have often thought how easy it would be to adapt and reserve part of a reservoir fishery for our less fortunate friends who may have had their love of fishing brought to a tragic end by some form of severe disability; we should always look for ways of providing these facilities. It is important to understand that opportunities for reservoir fishing are available upon payment and the observation of rules and regulations. To the Board or Water Company water is the most valuable commodity in the reservoir. Fishing, sailing, bird watching and other recreational facilities must be financed and run as separate functions and they are quite distinct and secondary to the main purpose of providing the consumer with a steady supply of wholesome water at reasonable cost. The cost of trout fishing in reservoirs varies considerably throughout the British Isles and each fishery has its rules covering conduct and fishing methods. On some waters fishing is by a full season permit only with facilities for guest permits in addition, but the majority of reservoirs offer trout fishing by day permit. There may be variations to cover weekly or part-seasonal periods also. Reductions in charges are sometimes available to younger fishermen and in some cases special charges are arranged for more senior anglers qualifying for pensions. Charges are often reduced if fishing is delayed until late afternoon. This is a particularly helpful arrangement for the fisherman who wants to get in an evening's fishing at the end of a day's work. In very general terms trout fishing in lakes and reservoirs is less expensive in the country-side of Scotland, Ireland and Wales, and the cost seems to increase as one gets within reasonable travelling distance of the larger towns, particularly in England. Due to inflation and frequent price revisions it will not help to give examples of reservoir fishing costs in detail because these are constantly under review and any individual costs will most probably be out of date before publication. If you think in terms of between £3 and £6 per day as at 1979 you should find a broad variety of very good fisheries within these figures. Appendix A includes advice as to where and to whom you should write for obtaining up to date information on fishing costs.

When considering day permits the term 'per day' needs a little explanation. Local rules must be studied but in some cases fishing starts at sunrise and is permitted until one hour after sunset. In other cases you may fish between fixed times, perhaps 8 am until 10.30 pm, and there are other variations which must be noted carefully wher-ever you decide to fish. In a superb book, *Still Water Fly Fishing* by T. C. Ivens, published by André Deutsch in 1970, chapter nineteen provides a first-class directory covering numerous reservoirs, lakes and still water fisheries in various regions as well as the addresses to which one should write for information for trout fishing facilities. I make no apology for more references to Mr Ivens' book during the following chapters because he has covered the entire sphere of reser-voir fishing in a most comprehensive and practical manner.

So much for notes on charges and some brief advice where and how to obtain information on where to fish. But what of the fish? Chapter 2 gives some general notes about reservoir trout but under the heading of fishing opportunities a would-be trout fisherman may like to know something about the quality of fish which are caught in different reservoirs. While every fisherman likes to catch a big fish, it would be wrong for a beginner to start with the idea of getting enjoy-ment from catching large trout only. There are numerous reservoirs offering tremendous sport with fish averaging 1 lb to 1½ lb and in those reservoirs formed by flooding rich arable land you will have these plus fish of 6 lb and upwards. At Blagdon in Somerset the 1970 season produced the best results since fishing started there in 1904 with a remarkable average weight of 2 lb 7 oz out of 7,395 fish taken and of these 212 were over 4 lb in weight. At Grafham in the opening season of 1966 over 4,000 fish caught were between 2 and 3 lb, over 2,000 fish between 3 and 4 lb and over 1,000 fish between 4 and 5 lb, and so on until about 15 between 7 and 8 lb. This is an example of an exceptionally large and successful new reservoir but as we shall see, the bank fisherman has done a lot towards spoiling the precious shallow marginal waters and some of his careless ways have scared fish well away from normal casting distance. The weights and details of fish mentioned include those caught by our friends in the boats as well but there is no reason why a beginner in bank fishing can't eventually learn to catch a fine specimen trout. Small trout of ¾ lb will give tremendous sport on fine tackle and ten minutes with a large rainbow trout will give you all the excitement you can hope for.

At the newly flooded reservoir at Bough Beech between Sevenoaks and Edenbridge, Kent, trout found an abundance of feed and for the first season in 1970 the best brown trout weighed 2 lb 14 oz and the best rainbow 4 lb 13 oz. More recently some fine specimen rainbow and brown trout above 6 lbs have been caught in this well managed fishery.

The enjoyment of reservoir trout fishing should not be thought of in terms of either the number or the weight of fish you catch. There is so much to be gained in bank fishing, particularly if you are prepared to be mobile and explore the less fished parts. You can learn to stalk rising fish and even if the fishing is a bit quiet on 'off' days there is a great deal of enjoyment to be had in discovering the ways and hiding places of fine birds and other creatures who settle in to reservoir surroundings.

What about the rules and regulations governing bank fishing? In the first place they vary from one fishery to another but here are the sort of things you can expect to find covered in most cases:

1. There is usually a map at the fishing lodge and referred to in the regulations and this must be studied carefully. It will show the roads or lanes in and away from the reservoir area, car parking areas, toilet facilities and shelters around the reservoir perimeter. Some maps have very valuable information about deep and shallow water, and as we shall see later these areas will affect our fishing methods.

2. Prices of permits and where they may be obtained.

3. In some cases, in addition to a reservoir fishing permit you will need a licence from the appropriate Water Authority.

4. Permits are not transferable and must be produced on request to any authorized person.

5. Nothing must be done which might cause pollution of water or vegetation on the reservoir banks.

6. Dogs are usually forbidden into reservoir premises.

7. Shooting, trapping or interference with any wild life is forbidden.

8. Precautions must be taken against the spread of fish disease by using the disinfectant provided in tanks at various points of entry. The disinfection of tackle and waders is essential.

9. Bathing and the use of radio sets are forbidden and everything possible must be done to avoid leaving litter.

10. The times for starting and finishing fishing are always defined.

11. Areas excluded from fishing are clearly indicated by map or notice boards.

12. Advice is generally given upon the danger spots, and anglers are reminded that wading must be done carefully and can be dangerous.

13. Anglers are prohibited from discarding nylon waste. The reason for this is that a tangle of nylon can cause suffering and death to birds and wild creatures.

14. The minimum strength of nylon permitted in use is generally specified. This will depend on the weight of fish in the reservoir.

15. The number of takeable fish will be given. Perhaps six or eight fish above 12" in length when measured from the snout to the fork of the tail. The taking of limit bags is not usually a problem for a beginner to worry about.

16. Instructions as to the returning or killing of undersized fish. Some Boards require all fish to be killed after hooking whilst others recommend the gentle release of undersized fish. Any angler having killed a number of takeable fish must pack up for the day.

17. All anglers must record their catches on the forms provided—including nil returns. Without this correct information it is not possible to keep proper records for stocking.

18. The Board reserves the right to cancel all fishing at any time without refund of payment.

19. Anglers fish entirely at their own risk and the reservoir authority are in no way responsible for any kind of loss or claim.

20. The permit covers 'fly fishing only'. Just what this phrase means

has formed the subject of many books but it excludes any form of bait fishing, the use of floats, spinning and other ingenious methods best left for the poacher. This book will describe the various methods of fly fishing which are permitted from the banks of reservoirs.

These rules may look a bit formidable at first sight but if you look at them in more detail they boil down to the application of common sense. Every sport has its own laws and reservoir trout fishing cannot be excepted.

Whilst it is always essential to know the rules of the reservoir you are fishing it is very worth while having a chat with the bailiff before you start fishing. He is the man who can provide you with help and guidance as to where you are likely to find good sport during progress of the season. He knows every inch of the shore line and can warn you where there may be soft and dangerous mud or perhaps an old tree stump in deep water which will lead to tangles and wasted time if you fish near it. If you explain you are a beginner it is more than likely that he will give you a few tips and a feeling of confidence which will help you to success. A good bailiff makes for a good atmosphere at a reservoir. He can introduce you to new friends and in my experience you find that where a reservoir is well controlled by the bailiff and his assistants the fishing prospers for the benefit of all who pay to fish it.

This chapter has given an introduction to the beginner as to why and where reservoirs are, the opportunities for fishing them and the sort of rules you must keep to in the majority of cases. Photographs 1, 2, 3 and 4 facing pages 16 and 17 show the reservoir at Bough Beech first opened as a trout fishery in May 1970. This reservoir was formed by damming the southern end of an arable valley beneath Ide Hill and the whole project is generally acclaimed as being entirely in keeping with the soft Kentish countryside and of great visual amenity.

Approaches to bank fishing

We have seen the sort of opportunities which may occur when a new reservoir is built, and in the older, well-established reservoirs trout fishermen have enjoyed their fishing for many years past. What are the approaches to this kind of fishing? Boat fishing apart, there are really two types of bank fishermen. First there is the one who knows the trout's feeding grounds in a certain area and he covers a wide area of water by skilled long-distance casting, making a methodical search at different depths but remaining fairly static in his own fishing position. Second there is the bank fisherman who prefers to travel very light and explore the rather less fished and more distant parts of the reservoir, trying here and there and moving on. It is entirely a matter of temperament as to which style you adopt but it is important to know that to a considerable extent the style you choose will have a bearing on the type of tackle you'll need. If you are a complete beginner it will pay to go to your reservoir with a fishing friend before buying much tackle. You will have the benefit of seeing the different methods of bank fishing and the different types of fishermen who, for the want of a better description, I refer to as the static types and roaming types.

To be successful at reservoir fishing you need to learn many different ways of deceiving the trout and in order to bring these different methods to good effect it will pay to be adaptable to a change in tactics as and when conditions dictate. There is no element of purism in this type of fishing, in other words we do not need to waste hours waiting for a fish to show before casting to him; we keep casting at different depths until we find a taker and in my style of fishing—the roaming type—I keep on the move looking for as many likely holding grounds as I can cover in the course of a day's fishing. Neither need we pay too much attention to the exact imitation of natural flies or other creatures in the tying of the artificial flies we use, because the greater part of the art of bank fishing for reservoir trout lies in presenting a fish with an artificial of the right size at the correct depth and imparting a little life-like movement into the artificial by working both rod and line in such a manner as to deceive the trout into making a mistake. When trout are showing at the surface then we fish for them in the upper water and when there are no signs of fish feeding or moving we search for them by altering our fishing methods to suit the varying depths of water which we regard as being likely holding grounds for the trout. To supplement the art of using rod, line and fly we must learn how trout behave under different conditions of weather and light, their favourite feeding grounds in various types of reservoirs and the variety of small creatures and insects which they devour. We must study the different types of shore and opportunities for successful fishing throughout the season and learn to use the different types of tackle which will best serve our needs for bank fishing. Whichever style of bank fishing you finally select as giving the most enjoyment, accept the fact that there are bound to be blank days and many of them. Experts with years of experience have them so it is inevitable that the beginner should have his share. Remember too that in the early days of a newly opened fishery the trout will often be caught without too much skill on the part of the angler. As time goes by the fish will become harder to deceive and in established reservoirs there are many fine trout who know a lot about fly fishing—enough at any rate to avoid being deceived too easily. As you acquire more knowledge about his life in a reservoir you will find it pays to consider matters from the trout's point of view because in this sport it helps if you can imagine what a trout is likely to be doing under different seasonal conditions. By thinking along these lines we plan our tactics for deceiving him, and that's what it's all about.

2

The Trout We Hope to Catch

Reservoirs are stocked with trout which have been reared in hatcheries at fish farms. The young fish of perhaps 8"–10" in size are delivered and carefully released from special containers, perhaps twenty-five at a time into their new surroundings, and put in at various points around the shore line and from boats into the outer water areas also. Many of the older established reservoirs have their own hatcheries where the trout are bred and cared for until ready for stocking. The breeding and rearing of trout is a highly skilled business and a great deal of research goes on during its process. The sizes of trout used for stocking vary from one reservoir to another and the stocking programme is arranged both during and out of the fishing season. The numbers and sizes of fish put in will depend upon the area of water and availability of natural feed to sustain them. In some reservoirs fish of 2 lb or more in weight are included in the stocking programme, and there are no hard and fast rules as to how many fish are put in per acre of water as each reservoir varies in its capacity to support their growth. Trout rarely breed naturally in reservoirs, as they need free running and well oxygenated water over gravel or shingle for their spawning beds, and these conditions are seldom available in reservoirs founded on impervious subsoil.

In layman's terms our trout are of two types—the Brown and the Rainbow. There are different sub species but these need not worry us. The brown trout has descended from his relatives who are the natives of our rivers but the rainbow trout is a quite different species, not a native of the British Isles but imported many years ago from the west of North America. The rainbow trout does not breed very well in the rivers of this country and there are few rivers in which he has established himself and reproduced naturally. The rainbow trout is of immense value for reservoir stocking because although he only lives about half as long as a brown trout he grows about twice as fast and is therefore cheaper for rearing to a catchable size. Brown trout continue to grow throughout their lifetime and can reach a much larger size than a rainbow. The weight of a brown trout is controlled by the availability of feed and it is possible to have one four years old weighing four pounds and another of the same age weighing no more than a pound—with both fish in very good condition. Rainbows grow rapidly where rich feed is available but reach their peak much faster, being at their best as two year olds or so when they might weigh as much as 6 lb. A brown trout of the same age and feeding under similar conditions might weigh about 3 lb. Brown trout can live for many years and reach a prodigious size depending upon food supply. Looking at some details in the 1971 edition of *Where to Fish* published by Harmsworth Press Ltd I see that in 1866 a brown trout of 39½ lb was caught on Loch Awe, foul hooked by a trout fly, and took a Mr W. Muir two and a half hours' work to land it. Probably we shall not have to contend with these sort of problems in our progress from the beginner stage but we must be prepared for the occasional trout of between six and seven pounds if our bank fishing takes place amongst the richer reservoirs. With the development of high protein feeding at specialised hatcheries it is most probable that trout of 20 lb or so may occasionally be encountered in a limited number of fisheries.

The trout's anatomy and senses
The trout may be described as a backboned being with fins instead of limbs and the ability to breathe in water. His breathing apparatus is designed so that he takes in water by his mouth from which it is passed through his gills. The gills contain tiny filaments which extract oxygen from the water and pass it into the blood stream. In rivers, the trout takes up a lie facing the current. If he faced the other way his gills would not work and he would drown. The brown trout is recognized by his brilliantly varied spots which range from light brown through to orange and gold. The rainbow trout has a beautiful purple sheen glazed over his more silvery spots. Both have great fighting power when hooked and a brown trout generally tries to

bore down fast and deep during his fight whereas the first rushes from a hooked rainbow are generally accompanied by some spectacular leaping and general thrashing about above the surface. Rainbows are prone to 'eye fluke' which can lead to blindness and when this occurs they become almost black in colour.

A trout's age is determined by a very skilled business of scale reading. This is an exact science, but if you catch a good fish and are interested in knowing its age the bailiff will most probably be the best man to ask. The trout has a built-in camouflage system which enables him to blend into his surroundings at any time. If you keep very quiet and wear a pair of polaroid glasses you can sometimes see your fish lurking around in the marginal weed beds, poised for instant movement towards their feed. They are most perfectly pro-

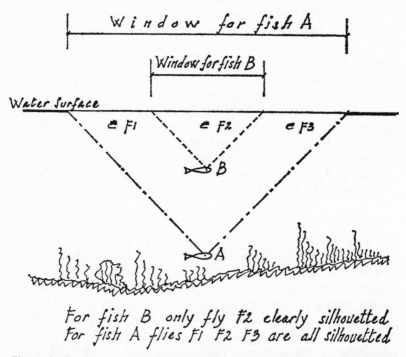

For fish B only fly F2 clearly silhouetted
For fish A flies F1 F2 F3 are all silhouetted

Figure 1. Trout have a 'window' of vision. In this example the flies would be silhouetted less sharply if there were a rippled surface. Therefore the fisherman has a better chance of deceiving a trout if he can present his fly beneath rippled water.

portioned fish with the ability to swim with lightning speed or to remain completely stationary. The trout's senses are of great importance to the fisherman. His eyes are on either side of his head and do not look just to the front like ours. He can see to left and right and above as well. If he is lying deep he can see an object behind his position. His vision is described as being contained within a 'window' and figure 1 shows in diagrammatic form the way in which he can see things at different depths. He can see a great deal if he is lying deep but very little when up near the surface. His view of objects sited on a level bank is poor when he is lying high in the water but better when he is deeper down—so if you are stalking trout feeding in the marginal weed beds get down on one knee for your casting to reduce the chances of his seeing you or being scared by your shadow. Except for direct vision in his window he sees what is going on beneath him by reflection from the water surface which acts as a huge mirror. His window of vision will be blurred under heavy ripple and in murky and cloudy conditions his vision is generally impaired because rays of light cannot easily penetrate the water. Our chances of deceiving him are therefore better when there is a ripple on the water because he loses some of his ability to see exactly whether he is taking a natural creature or a man-made imitation. He does not see well in brilliant sunlight—he has no eyelids and becomes dazzled—but he can pick out all kinds of creatures under darker conditions. We do not know a great deal about his ability to differentiate colours as we do, but he is certainly attracted by the flash or sheen caused when a smaller fish turns, and this influences the tying of a number of small fry imitations. He seems generally interested in artificials containing black, silver, gold and red and we shall study later the various types of artificials which are used in our reservoir fly fishing.

As for his hearing the trout is equipped with a most sensitive system which reacts instantly to any form of vibration. If you see a trout feeding near a weed bed it is probable that he would continue undisturbed if a gun were fired into the air above—but two clumsy footsteps towards the water will cause sufficient vibration to scare him out. Trout are tremendously sensitive to underwater vibration and one of the golden rules for successful bank fishing is to avoid wading into the valuable shallows whenever possible. Hundreds of acres of rich feeding grounds in shallow water have been ruined by

reservoir fishermen through clumsy wading; the result is that trout
are driven out, making long-distance casting the only approach where
this has happened. A beginner must avoid these heavily fished areas
and be prepared to wander up the reservoir to the more distant and
quieter parts where the trout remain undisturbed amongst the marginal weed beds, because it is in such parts that you can learn so
many interesting ways of deceiving a trout at much closer quarters.

Hearing is mainly governed by the ability to sense vibrations of
different intensity. The trout's system is distributed along his 'lateral

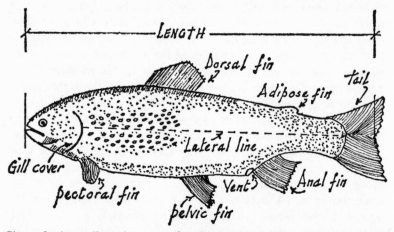

Figure 2. An outline of a trout. Length is measured from the snout to the
fork of the tail.

line'—this is the long line which extends along the centre of both
flanks of his body as indicated in figure 2, which provides an outline
of his general anatomy. Unlike his relations in rivers, who take up
lies facing the current and wait for it to bring food to them, the
reservoir trout must swim and look for it. Once trout settle into a
reservoir they take up a fairly regular pattern of cruising—usually
into the wind—and this pattern remains reasonably predictable until
there is a sudden change in weather conditions. A considerable part
of the reservoir fishing art, whether from rowing boat or bank,
centres around knowing where trout are likely to be at different times
of the season under varying weather conditions. Provided the trout
are left to their own devices they will work out cruising lines and
feeding grounds but any form of major disturbance will rapidly put

them off their normal routine. It is for this reason that on a small reservoir of about 250 acres as considered in chapter 1 sailing and fishing cannot take place at the same time. No matter how skilled the sailor, the bow waves from sailing craft will set up enough vibration to scare the trout out of his normal feeding and cruising habits, thus ruining the chances of successful fishing and reducing it to a matter of luck as opposed to the application of knowledge as to where and how to fish if the trout are left undisturbed. Rowing boat fishing for trout in the hands of a skilled boat fisherman will do nothing to upset the fish, but if the fisherman is one of less skill and of the type who ships his oars with a resounding thud and then proceeds to bang about on the bottom boards, then he too must accept his share of blame for causing the type of vibration which upsets parts of a fishery. It is impossible to pay too much regard to the trout's aversion to any form of vibration when considering reservoir fishing as a whole.

The trout is considered to have some limited sense of smell: he has buds in his nostrils and it seems that big old trout, although mainly blind, who feed mainly at night search out their food by some such sense. It seems probable that trout have a sense of taste— otherwise why should he devour a lucious blood worm but refuse a large insect which may taste 'sour' to him? The trout's sex life is rather repressed under reservoir conditions due to the lack of spawning beds. However, the female or hen fish and the male cock fish must shed their ova and milt respectively and as a result you may find trout in rather lanky condition during the early part of a season. Such fish are best returned if this can be done without harming them. Under reservoir conditions all fish are not able to shed eggs or milt and this can cause quite a high mortality rate in adult fish. If a hen fish becomes egg-bound her condition is described as 'gravid' and she sickens. The sexing of trout is a skilled business and particularly so in small fish. A large cock fish in prime condition is easily recognized by a small barb which extends up from his lower jaw, and the lower jaw protrudes beyond the upper one. A hen fish usually has a shorter head than a cock fish and the markings of a cock fish are generally more brilliant than those of the hen. A beginner need not worry about which sex of fish he has caught. The trout know which is which and this is all that really matters.

So far I have given an outline of how our different types of trout get into reservoirs and some notes on their physical make-up and senses. In a very light-hearted and pleasant book, *Fishing the Dry Fly* by Dermot Wilson, published by A. & C. Black in 1970, the author writes of the alleged cunning and brain power of the trout as follows: 'You will often hear trout described as artful, cunning and resourceful. This is far too flattering. No trout thinks. His behaviour is usually dictated purely by instinctive responses, although these may have been influenced a little by his own experiences. If he takes the dry fly you offer him he does so because this is his response to something that looks like food when he is hungry. If he refuses it he does so because it does not look like the food he wants.' I am sure this is the case in reservoir fishing when a trout decides to take or refuse whatever type of artificial you may be fishing at the time. The photographs 5 and 6 facing page 32 show brown and rainbow trout taken from Bough Beech reservoir during the 1971 season weighing 2 lb 4 oz and 2 lb 9 oz respectively. There are many bigger, but you will have tremendous satisfaction when you have learnt to catch trout as good as these.

His reactions to the weather

Reservoirs and lakes are frequently referred to as 'still waters' but a huge volume of water is seldom, if ever, still in the literal sense. Sunshine causes convection currents which set up circulation, and wind playing across a large sheet of water can produce conditions varying from mild ripple to wild surf. Reservoir trout adopt settled habits of cruising and feeding which remain relatively unchanged until there is a sudden change in the weather. Squally winds upset normal cruising courses and in oppressive thundery weather the trout tend to skulk in the depths and become difficult to interest. After a sharp rain or hailstorm the water is re-oxygenated and the fish swim fast and rejoice. They will feed wildly in the slicks of foam which hold hundreds of insects suspended in the froth. Trout will rise to snowflakes and good catches have been recorded during snowstorms of early-season fishing. The fish like dull weather with gentle mild winds and occasional gleams of sunshine. They feed well under these conditions and the trout's vision is particularly sharp under a darker sky. Brilliant sun and blinding heat put the trout off surface feeding but you may be able to deceive him in the cooler deep water. Fish are generally active when the barometer is rising, but become less active as it falls. Gentle showers provide fresh oxygen, bright periods of warm sun encourage insect hatches and both these conditions set him feeding and cruising. Rolling mist or thick fog put him right off. The trout are particularly active at sunrise and again towards and after sunset, but a cold wind at the end of a warm day will usually put him off his evening feed in the upper water levels. He loves the weedly shallows but will move away from them when the water becomes too tepid and lacking in oxygen.

His feeding habits

He will be found amongst the weed beds in the shallows feeding on aquatic insects but will be rapidly scared away by clumsy wading or careless fishing methods. Newly flooded arable land will hold an abundance of bottom feed and in the early stages of a new reservoir of this type the tendency will be for the trout to feed heavily in the lower levels, but as the bottom feed lessons in quantity the trout will supplement his diet by aquatic insects, and land-bred insects blown from the banks out over the water. The trout likes rocky margins or the faces of a dam holding masses of water snail, and he will frequently be found feeding at the edge of rippled water because this is where offshore wind meets water, and any land-bred insects will be blown to this line. He usually cruises upwind because feed suspended in the surface film will be moving towards him. Following an overnight wind from west to east he may be found next morning working the eastern shore line sorting out last night's left-overs suspended in the froth. He will work hard searching for feed in scoured-out sections of a gravel embankment, and in shallow bays with plenty of weed he will nose out water boatmen, freshwater shrimps, snail and blood worm. He likes to lie out in deeper water perhaps ten yards from a feeder stream or ditch, where running fresh water enters the reservoir bringing an assortment of feed towards him. He can often be found lying in deep water next to a shallow shelf at the margins. In the shallows insects will be hatching, which he can move to and take at leisure, after which he returns to his less conspicuous position in the adjoining deep water. He will feed hard in rough water with foam slicks holding suspended insects and water creatures. He searches out and gorges stickleback, minnow and small fry, swimming high and fast in the water in a wild forage and scattering the small fish in all directions. Flooded hedgerows often harbour masses of stickleback and the trout will rapidly chase them out into different parts of the reservoir.

Perhaps the most important of all reservoir feeding grounds are to be found when 'calm lanes' occur. Referring again to *Still Water Fly Fishing* by T. C. Ivens, the author describes the importance of these areas in great detail. Very briefly these lanes are formed where the wind is divided by a copse or promontory and in consequence there is an unmistakable appearance of calm and rippled water as in photograph 7 facing page 33, reproduced by kind permission of Mr Ivens. Calm lanes lead to calm air and in these conditions trout may cruise or lie stationary beneath in the knowledge that insects will hatch in these undisturbed areas of quiet water. As a beginner you must always look for signs of calm lanes—preferably positioning yourself so that they are running approximately parallel to the shore so that you may fish the ripple edge of the lane as thoroughly as possible.

His visible movements

For a large part of the time spent on reservoir fishing you may not see any signs of fish at all. This is not to say they are not there to be caught, but deep water tactics are required and we shall learn about these later. On the other hand we are often able to see signs of a trout as he breaks the surface in the act of 'rising'. When he rises he does so in several different ways and it is important to recognize the different rise forms because they indicate separate types of feeding and may be summarized as follows:

1. A kidney-shaped whorl is usually associated with a rise to a large surface fly.

2. A sipping movement, by which a small 'hole' or 'dimple' appears in the water, usually indicates that a trout is lying in the upper level sucking surface insects down to him.

3. Sipping rises coupled with circular cruising usually indicates very selective feeding on small midges.

4. If you see a large tail appear above the water followed by a water explosion it is probable that a big trout has decided to swat his prey before mouthing it.

5. A leaping fish (provided he is not hooked) is probably having fun and not feeding.

6. A deliberate head and tail rise is usually to a surface insect which the trout takes on the way down.

Photograph 5. A brown trout of 2 lb 4 oz, 17" long. Markings of brown trout differ very considerably but they are usually pronounced, with richly coloured spots. This is a cock fish, identified by the protruding lower jaw with its up-turned barb

Photograph 6. A rainbow trout of 2 lb 9 oz, 18½" long. There are no pronounced spots but the markings usually create a fine sheen ranging from purple-pink to silver-green. Both the photographs on this page were provided by D. Mackinnon from a catch during the 1971 season at Bough Beech.

Above: Photograph 7. When calm lanes form amid ripple the bank fisherman must try to position himself so he can fish the ripple edge very carefully. Trout frequently cruise or lie stationary beneath calm lanes awaiting insect hatches which are encouraged by the calm air above the lanes.

Below: Photograph 8. When the wind sets into a dam or embankment trout will often search for scoured-out feed close to the water's edge. Good catches can sometimes be made by casting a short line and working the fly at different depths and speeds, but your casting position must be well back to avoid fish scaring. Both these photographs have been reproduced from *Still Water Fly Fishing* by kind permission of T. C. Ivens.

7. Tail wagging above shallow water indicates that the trout is nosing out weed beds or a muddy bottom in his search for feed.

8. A 'humping' or 'bulging' rise indicates that the trout is taking nymphs in the upper water level.

9. Wild foraging with the trout swimming high and fast in the water with the creation of a miniature bow wave means that he is chasing minnow, stickleback or other small fry.

As G. W. Maunsell summarizes in his comprehensive book, *The Fisherman's Vade Mecum*, fourth edition, published by A. & C. Black in 1967: 'A trout rises to a fly or takes a lure for one of the following reasons:

a. Hunger: because it appears like something good to eat.

b. Curiosity: it attracts him and he desires to investigate it.

c. Tyranny: it looks like something alive and in distress.

d. Jealousy: others in the pool may get it before him.'

His insect larder

There is no need for a beginner to learn much about fly life but for those who are interested in this aspect of fly fishing it will be helpful to know a little about the insects which are of importance to the trout. Some reservoirs, particularly those in upland and rocky regions, have little bottom feed when compared to those formed by flooding arable land. In the former type the trout will depend more upon aquatic and land-bred insects for his feed, but in both types of reservoir the insects will be available for him if he wants them. We shall see in chapter 6 that a number of fishermen's flies are tied to give a degree of imitation to the naturals for occasions when the trout are thought to be feeding on blood worms, water snails, shrimp, small fish and other delicacies forming part of the trout's diet. In his masterly book, *Trout Flies of Still Water* published by A. & C. Black in 1969, the author John Goddard writes: 'The entomological orders of Ephemeroptera, Diptera, Trichoptera and Plecoptera include many of the insects which are of importance to the fly-fisherman, and for simplicity these orders can be described as Upwinged flies, Flat-winged flies, flies with Roof-shaped wings, and Hard-winged flies. The latter are of less importance to the still water fisherman than the previous three.' Photographs 9–12 facing page 48 are reproduced from this excellent book and shows an example of each type of fly.

A very informative article was written by Dr Digby Lewis and

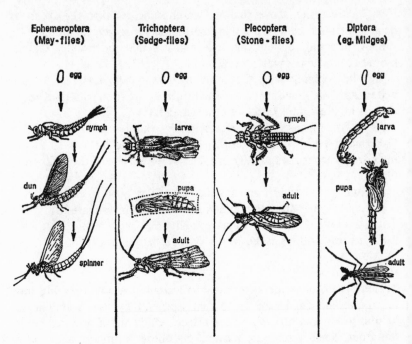

Figure 3. Development from egg to adult in four groups of insects of particular interest to the reservoir trout. Reproduced by kind permission of Dr Digby Lewis from his article 'The Trout's Larder' published in the June 1970 edition of *Trout and Salmon* magazine.

published in the June 1970 edition of *Trout and Salmon* and figure 3 reproduced from that article shows the stages of development from egg to adult in each of the four groups of insects to which Mr Goddard refers. The Upwinged flies, e.g. mayflies, have a segmented body, two or three long tails and very upright wings. Flies with Roof-shaped wings, e.g. sedge flies, are rather moth-like in appearance without tails, and when at rest the hairy soft wings are closely folded to give a long triangular appearance. The Flat-winged flies, e.g. midges, are without tails and generally have fairly short transparent wings. The Hard-winged flies, e.g. stoneflies, have long shiny wings and when at rest these are folded flat. In reservoirs the trout devour insects at various stages of their life and the Upwinged flies and Hard-winged flies are frequently taken at their nymphal stage. A nymph is a small legged creature bearing some resemblance to the adult insect but is without wings. Flies with Roof-shaped wings and the Flat-winged flies make two important changes during their early life of interest to the trout. The first is from egg to larva and the second from larva to pupa. Nymphs, midge pupae, sedge larvae and pupae are devoured in huge quantities by the trout and because of this it will pay the fisherman to use artificials giving some resemblance to these creatures in order to deceive the trout when he is known to be concentrating on this type of feed. In addition to the water-bred insects, others are frequently blown from the reservoir banks onto the water surface and of these the hawthorn fly, black gnat, winged ants and bracken beetles are of great interest to the trout cruising along the ripple edge, because it is on this line, where the wind meets water that these and other land-bred insects will fall.

His enemies

He probably has many but here are some examples:

1. Little trout are very scared of big trout and must keep their distance to avoid being chased and eaten.

2. Herons cause severe injury by spearing but failing to kill and eat their prey.

3. Cormorants who find their way in from the coast to sample a fresh water fish for a change.

4. Fish disease, in particular that abbreviated to UDN and which every reservoir fisherman must co-operate in preventing by the disinfecting of waders and other tackle whenever called upon to do so.

5. Poachers.

6. Noisy boat fishermen and clumsy bank fishermen who scare him by causing severe vibration.

7. Careful fishermen if they are clever enough to deceive him.

When he is caught

Later on we shall study suitable tactics for catching our fish but once he has been hooked and brought to the net, follow these actions:

1. If he is obviously above the size limit kill him instantly by two or three sharp blows across the skull.

2. If it is doubtful whether he is up to the size limit leave the fish in the net just in the water and check his length without touch-

ing him. If he is to be released ease the hook and return him un-touched.

3. If he is undersized and bleeding from any part, kill him.

4. If he is undersized and slightly hooked bring him towards you by raising the rod vertical, run your thumb and finger down to the hook-hold just at water level, give a quick jerk with your wrist and the fish will swim free.

Never handle a fish which is to be returned to the water because your hands will remove his protective slime and damage his scales. If a fish is to be handled do so by wetting your hands first, and if he is to be returned after handling do so gently by setting him on a level keel and if possible with his head into the wind. If you have the slightest doubt that you may have caught a diseased or injured fish kill him and show the fish to the bailiff.

Cleaning and cooking

One of the easiest ways of cleaning a trout is to lay him on his back on a board with his vent pointing up. Insert a sharp thin knife into the vent and slit him from the vent right up to the vee of the gills. Open the fish and the insides will come away cleanly. Scrape out any remains and flush out with cold water. Leave the head and tail on unless he is too big for the pot.

There are many ways of cooking trout but here are my favourites:

1. Baking in aluminium foil with a knob of butter inside the fish.

2. Grilling. Particularly good with small fish.

3. Steaming in salted water. Leave to cool, then put the fish in the 'fridge for an hour or two and serve with salad and mayonnaise.

4. Smoked on a special smoking outfit available at good tackle shops.

3

Tackle, Clothing and Other Equipment

The object of this chapter is to summarize items under the above headings and to give some idea of probable cost. Technicalities of tackle design and manufacture are purposely avoided. When buying tackle it is essential to obtain advice from and deal with first-class manufacturers. They are aware of the growing popularity of reservoir fishing and retain the services of some very experienced fishermen to advise them; Such names as Hardy, Farlow, Dermot Wilson, Fordham, Garcia, Gladding, Bruce and Walker, Sealey or Intrepid can be heard during discussions between fishermen on most reservoirs and there are many other first-class firms specializing in reservoir tackle design throughout the country.

Before buying tackle, ask a fisherman or the bailiff of a reservoir you intend to fish for names of manufacturers whose goods are in use in your locality. Write to the manufacturers, explain you are a beginner and ask their advice as to suitable tackle for your needs. Make it clear that you want value for money. A good manufacturer should follow up a detailed enquiry with a personal letter plus catalogue and also refer you to their nearest stockist in your district. Take a fisherman friend to the tackle shop and be guided by what he has to say. Do not rush into this business of buying tackle, it needs careful selection. You do not know at this stage whether you are going to really enjoy this new sport, so spend moderately.

Choosing and buying tackle may be done in two ways, as you can either buy brand new or second hand. In the priced items which follow later in this chapter I have allowed for purchasing good quality new tackle as manufactured by reliable firms and retailed either by them direct or through their authorized agents. I make this qualification because as an alternative to the specialist tackle shop there are large department stores who sell fishing tackle as well as a multitude of other goods ranging from household furnishings to food, and whilst the tackle in such stores may be all right, it will be better for a beginner to purchase from the tackle specialist. It is quite easy to buy sound second hand tackle provided you deal with a reliable firm and above all be guided by a fisherman friend so that he may check the quality and suitability of the items on your behalf. The most competitive prices for new tackle are mainly on goods imported from Japan, and substantial savings below the approximate costs given later may be made if you purchase Japanese tackle. The main point to keep in mind is that you must be guided by an experienced reservoir fisherman when you are choosing tackle of any kind and at any price range. The most important items of tackle are the fly rod, reel and line. They will most probably be the three most expensive also—so let's consider a few details.

1. Rod

The ideal rod for a beginner must be light enough to permit long periods of use without tiring him and powerful enough to permit accurate casting up to about 20 yards. With gradual skill he will increase on this distance but for real long distance casting, around the 40-yard mark, he will require specially designed tackle, and the long distance school is not the best training ground for the beginner who must concentrate on accuracy and casting form. Distance comes later. It is not essential to cast great distances to catch fish from the quieter and less popular stretches of reservoir banks. Unfortunately it has been made so on a number of reservoirs through clumsy wading and careless fishing methods, causing fish to move off away from the shallows, but where this has occurred trout can still be caught close to the margins in the more distant and less fished parts.

Fly rods are made from two principal materials, built cane and hollow fibre glass. A built cane rod is more expensive mainly due to the basic price of high quality material cane imported for this purpose, plus the very skilled and costly labour involved. A cane rod is solid, and hexagonal in cross section with a gradual taper from butt to tip. Hollow fibre glass is tubular in section and recent developments of manufacture have led to some excellent rods in this material. A suitable rod will probably be about nine feet in length and be of two sections joined by suction ferrules. Rods are described as having a certain type of 'action'. This refers to the manner by which a rod is able to flex under tension. Tension in the action of casting is created by the weight of the fly line travelling behind or in front of the rod tip. It is necessary that your first rod should respond throughout its length from tip to butt as this will facilitate easier casting. When a rod's action is felt from tip to butt it is described as having an 'all through' action. Some rods are specially designed to have a pronounced tip action whilst others are very rigid. The latter are not suitable for a beginner. Fishermen become very attached to their favourite rod and a really good built cane rod which has been carefully looked after can last a lifetime, but all good manufacturers are producing high-quality hollow glass rods at competitive prices and these are admirable for both beginner and experienced fishermen. Photographs 13 and 15 facing page 49 show parts of two rods suitable for reservoir bank fishing. The latest carbon-fibre rods are excellent but I do not recommend them for a beginner for the reasons explained in my Introduction.

2. *Reel*

Your reel must be matched to suit the rod, and be simple in design, smooth-running and easy to take apart. A line guard is essential to protect the plastic coating of the fly line. The reel must be capable of holding a 30-yard standard fly line of the size and weight indicated on the rod butt plus at least 50 yards of terylene backing. If your reservoir holds large and powerful fish then the length of the backing must be increased and this will mean a reel of larger diameter. Reels can be adapted for either left or right hand wind. Many reels are sold with a spare spool on which you may carry a second line of an alternative type. Photograph 14 facing page 49 shows a traditional reel and a good quality floating line in its package.

3. *Fly lines*

There are two main types: *a.* those designed to float on the water; *b.* those designed to sink beneath it.

Both are usually of 30-yard length and contain an inner core with a plastic coated dressing. The type of core depends on whether the line is required to sink or float. Lines are designated by a scale known as the AFTM scale (Association of Fishing Tackle Manufacturers).

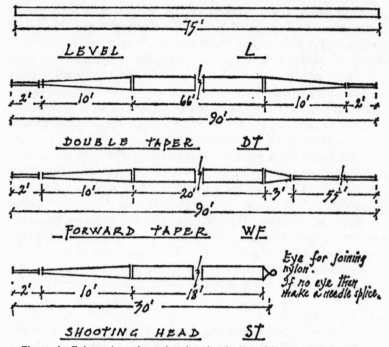

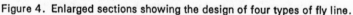

Figure 4. Enlarged sections showing the design of four types of fly line.

This scale includes a series of numbers from 1–12 which refer to the weight of the line. No. 1 is the lightest and No. 12 the heaviest. The AFTM scale describes a line by reference to the weight of the first 30 feet excluding its level tip and the AFTM number will be on the box of every new fly line.

Floating lines are manufactured in different colours, usually ivory or very light green. Ivory is the rather better colour for floating lines because they are easier to see by the fisherman and less so by the trout. Sinking lines are usually green or of darkish colour and are less visible to fish against a dark deep water background. Fly lines are further classified as being double taper, forward taper, shooting head or level. Level lines are little used for reservoir fishing although the lighter ones may be adapted for backing purposes. Figure 4 shows in diagrammatic form four types of fly line, adapted from an excellent booklet, *To Cast a Trout Fly* published by Messrs Farlow's and Hardy Brothers in conjunction with Scientific Anglers Inc. of America.

Advantages of each line

DOUBLE TAPER: The advantage of this type is that after an amount of wear it can be turned end for end and should therefore have a longer life. It is a good line to use when bank fishing where fish may be covered without need for long distance casting.

FORWARD TAPER: This type assists in obtaining more distance for the same effort and is particularly helpful for pushing a line through the difficult winds which so frequently crop up during reservoir fishing. The thin shooting line which follows the heavy forward taper creates very little air resistance.

SHOOTING HEAD: A shooting head outfit usually consists of 30 feet of fly line similar in profile and weight to a forward taper line. Most shooting heads are provided with a loop for joining the backing, which usually consists of about 100 yards of nylon mono-filament of about 25–30 lb breaking strain. This nylon backing creates the minimum of frictional resistance as it travels through the rod rings during casting, and the use of a shooting head coupled with a style of casting known as the 'double haul' will enable a skilled fisherman to cast 40 yards or more regularly, but this technique is not included in the beginner's syllabus. Shooting heads are consistently used by fishermen preferring to adopt the long distance casting technique but they are not suitable for a complete beginner. They must be matched in weight to the type of rod and may be of floating or sinking quality as tactics demand. Some reservoir regulations forbid the use of shooting heads and it may be desirable to restrict their use, particularly on smaller waters where fish may be covered by the standard forward taper or double taper fly line. The use of a shooting head is an admirable approach when fish cannot be reached by other means and a successful reservoir fisherman must be sufficiently adaptable in his approach to make full use of the shooting head technique after he has learnt fully the correct methods of casting the traditional 30-yard fly line.

A new fly line package will have a code marking made up as follows:

DT double taper   S sinking
WF forward taper (i.e. weight forward)   F floating
ST shooting taper (i.e. shooting head)

and there will also be a number which relates to the weight of the first 30 feet. Your line may therefore be classified as DT-6-F, i.e.

double taper No. 6 floating line, or WF-7-S, i.e. forward taper No. 7 sinking line. Always remember that your rod *must* be matched to the correct *weight* of line and this weight will be indicated by the AFTM marking above the rod handle. The marking will look like this: # 6 indicating that your rod should be matched to a No. 6 line. If you acquire a rod without a number marked above the handle take it to a first-class tackle dealer and ask him to prescribe a suitable line weight. Earlier rod patterns are not so marked. Photograph 16 facing page 49 shows an enlargement of the AFTM markings on two types of rod.

A beginner should start with a forward taper floating fly line. This will enable him to feel and develop the power in his rod without the need for getting out a long length of line. It is true that for catching fish during the earlier part of the season a sinking line would be more appropriate, because fish will generally be lying deep, but for the first month of the season our beginner should forget about catching fish and concentrate on getting his rod and line to work correctly, so that when the fish start rising in about May, he has acquired sufficient casting skill to cover them accurately. A floating line will assist him in his casting because it will lift off from the water surface without any obstruction, whereas a sinking line cannot be brought sharply up for the back cast until all but a few feet of line tip have been fully retrieved. Any attempt to draw out a submerged length of sunk line will completely overstrain any rod and may quite easily break it.

Assuming you buy brand new tackle from first-class manufacturers the cost of our three principal items rounded up to the nearest pound sterling at 1979 prices may look something like this:

	£
*9′ 0″ hollow glass two-piece reservoir rod	26
Intrepid reel and spare spool	10
†McHardys Mill end floating line	3
	39

* e.g. Bucknall "Two-Lakes" or Fordham "Hornet".
† Mill end lines have very slight imperfections but I have used them for several years and you can have three good Mill end lines for the price of one top quality line. For full details write to McHardys of Carlisle.

If you are unable to resist the temptation of buying a built cane rod this will add about another £25 and if you want a 30-yard sinking line right from the beginning then add about £5 more. Substantial savings can be made if carefully selected second hand goods are chosen and as previously mentioned, Japanese tackle will be the cheapest of all.

Next come some more essential but less expensive items as follows:

BACKING: This is usually of tough, rot-proof braided terylene, spliced to the fly line. There must be sufficient backing wound on to the reel spool, so that when the line is fully retrieved it just fills the reel drum and leaves clearance between line and the rim of the reel. About 50 to 75 yards of backing is generally adequate.

LEADERS: These are made from lengths of nylon tied to various patterns to link the fly (or flies) to the fly line. You will often hear fishermen referring to this nylon as a 'cast'. I use the word 'leader' right through this book because it is being used more frequently and the term 'leader' cannot be confused with the action of making a cast with a fly line or casting to a fish. It pays to make up your own leaders by buying about six spools each containing 25 yards of different diameters and breaking strains as recommended in chapter 4.

Knotless leaders are available made of continuous nylon extruded to give a gradually diminishing taper from the butt (i.e. the thick end) to the point. These are rather expensive but excellent under some conditions, particularly when fishing through weed where knots in leaders tend to become clogged. Leaders are best kept wound onto circular plastic carriers which in turn fit into a circular shaped box. Cheaper alternatives lie in winding them round pieces of thin sheet cork nicked with a razor blade to house the ends of nylon and better still, beer mats from the local pub make very good leader carriers in the same way.

LANDING NET: There is no need for great expense here. Collapsible, extending or folding nets are not generally the best for reservoir bank fishing as they are apt to become entangled or stuck by their own mechanism. A reservoir net should have a light alloy frame with a gape of at least 18 inches and a stout net with a depth of at least 24 inches. A one-piece handle about three feet long, marked with a 12-inch notch for fish measurement will be adequate for the job. The net in photograph 32 facing page 80 is home made and has a stout bamboo handle secured to the net frame, with a brass union housed in fibre glass. A stout cord and dog leash clip enable the net to be slung whilst fishing, and the end of the handle is fitted with a brass thread to receive either a rubber end stopper or a spade, so that if required the net handle can be stuck into the reservoir bed while fishing. It is very easy to make some form of quick release sling: one bridge ring, some stout cord and a dog leash are the essential items. The deep net is folded over the net frame when walking, thus keeping it clear of the ground and preventing the mesh getting caught up in brambles etc. Nets with a similar frame can be bought fitted to a 3′ 0″ alloy tube with an end stopper. These are very light and serviceable but the bright alloy must be etched and painted over to avoid flash during a bright day. Fish are easily scared by flash from the bank whether caused by bright metal or a very highly varnished rod.

FLY BOXES: Do not buy expensive clip-in boxes. They tend to damage fly dressings and can break small hook barbs. Alloy cigarette tins or cigar boxes are excellent. Line them with white polystyrene as this gives a light background and perfect hook hold. I use one box for wet flies and lures, one tin for nymphs and one tin or plastic box for dry flies. The dry fly box wants to be deeper so that the flies can sit upright with lid clearance. One box of flies will be adequate for our beginner.

FLIES: These are dealt with in some detail in chapter 6, but a beginner should buy no more than one dozen assorted and well tried lure, wet fly, and nymph patterns. The more you buy, the more time you will waste in making unnecessary changes which could be better devoted to fishing. For the whole of the 1964 season I stuck to four patterns only: The Black and Peacock Spider, Jersey Herd, Green Nymph and Brown Nymph. I learned to fish them as recommended by T. C. Ivens, and despite great temptation to try others I persevered with these four patterns in different hook sizes and gradually succeeded in catching several good fish. Reservoir fishing is just as any other sport—you must put in plenty of hard graft and practice for good results. Fortunately there is a fair element of 'beginner's luck' without which many of us would have given up years ago.

FISHING BAG: Again there is no need for expense. The larger the bag you have the greater will be the tendency to carry all kinds of rubbish not essential for the job. If I am fishing for a few hours I never carry a bag. But if I am out for the day, then a small ex-Army bag treated with silicone to make it waterproof is sufficient to hold thermos, snacks and some of the less essential but useful items listed later.

WAIST BAG: A small waist bag as photograph 34 facing page 81 is excellent. This is made by my daughter out of waterproof material, rather on the lines of a large purse with a generous flap which secures itself on contact by means of 'Velcro' strips. A slot at the back of the bag allows a leather waist belt to pass through. This bag holds fly boxes, blunt nose scissors on a lanyard threaded to the belt, a tin of Mucilin (a grease for making leaders float), a small box with soft cloth soaked in detergent (used for removing grease from leaders) and a small bottle of silicone used for making dry flies waterproof for as long as needed.

PRIEST: This is the tool for killing your fish and so named for administering last rites. There are some very elaborate ones for sale in tackle shops but there is certainly no need to spend much on this item. A piece of hard wood dowel with a strip of sheet lead tacked to the top is very useful, particularly if the handle is painted white when it will show up in the dark if you leave it on the bank. The old type of Rawlplug tool handle is also very good and I have used one of these for the past few years.

Our supplementary budget at 1979 prices may look like this:

	£
Line backing—75 yards	2·00
Leaders made from six spools 25 yard nylon—average cost per spool 50p—6 spools	3·00
Landing net (home-made)	5·00
Fly boxes (home-made)	0·50
Lures, wet flies and nymphs—1 dozen assorted	2·50
Waist bag (make one like mine)	1·00
Tin of Mucilin	0·50
*Detergent pad (and leader sinking mixture)	0·25
Scissors	2·00
Fly floatant (you won't need this until you become interested in dry fly fishing)	0·50
Fisning bag (if you really need one)	5·00
Priest (home-made)	0·30

* A mixture of Fullers earth and washing up liquid makes a fine grey paste which can be wiped on to a leader to make it sink immediately.

Plastic bags for fish and clean rag for wiping hands   0·00
Beer mats for winding on leaders   0·00
                                                              ────
                                                            £22·55

                                                    say £23·00

If you buy brand new tackle from first-class firms, the financial position up to now will look like this:

	£
Expensive items (hollow glass rod, reel, spare spool, floating line and sinking line)	44
Supplementary items	23
	──
	67
say	70
	──

You must update these prices, which are based on 1979 costs, but remember the ways of making substantial savings previously mentioned and in particular the opportunities for buying good second hand tackle from reputable tackle shops.

Some more useful but not essential items

These may include a pair of artery forceps for tightening knots and removing obstinate hooks, polaroid glasses to prevent headaches caused by glare and to help see into the depths, a small torch is invaluable after sunset—a special long spoon for scooping a trout's gullet will often produce valuable evidence of what the fish are feeding on and the use of a spoon and small magnifier can give valuable information which may set you on the right tactics for deceiving a good fish. Circular white leader carriers are good value and will help to avoid tangles which otherwise occur when leaders are stuffed into your pocket. But you might leave out all these items in the hope that you will eventually acquire them as Christmas or birthday presents.

Clothing

If it is warm enough to fish with your jacket off always wear drab-coloured clothing beneath. There is not much point in standing out like a lighthouse when you are trying to get a little background cover for fishing close in.

FISHING JACKET: A fishing jacket must be light-weight and drab in colour. It should have a fitted hood, large pockets, be large fitting and of sufficient length to overlap the tops of your waders. All seams must be sealed. A removable lining is desirable but not essential. Fastenings must be simple and reliable. Zips, 'Velcro' or stout press studs are ideal.

WADERS: Tough industrial rubber waders with rubber soles are adequate for the greater part of reservoir fishing. Studded soles and heels add to cost but are essential if your reservoir contains large margins of rock or where fishing is permitted from the slope of a dam. Weed on rock or concrete causes slipperiness and studs or other safety soles are needed in these cases. Choose waders one size larger than normal shoes and fit a pair of felt innersoles.

WELLINGTONS: Tough knee-high wellingtons are all right for some reservoir banks where wading is unnecessary.

SOCKS: A pair of woollen socks under another of stout nylon provide warmth and the nylon takes the heavy wear without holes.

NECK TOWEL: A strip of old bath-towel is the best bad weather seal between your neck and the jacket collar. Scarves are no good.

HEADGEAR: A comfortable cap is a good all-rounder. Woolly caps are good during cold and fit snugly under a raised hood. These are particularly appreciated if you are mainly bald like me. There are some very exotic models of headgear available as presents later on— deer stalkers in tweed, or fancy patterns in waterproofed nylon.

MAIN CLOTHING COSTS: £

Jacket without detachable lining   22
Industrial rubber waders (without studded soles)   18
Extra cost of studded soles if essential   6
                                                                          ____

                                                                            46
                                                                          ____

So if you buy good quality new tackle, clothing and basic equipment the total outlay will probably amount to about £120 and having spent this sum you should be all set and ready to start, but do not forget to reserve the cost of your fishing permit and do remember the ways of effecting substantial savings by buying second hand goods under guidance from an experienced reservoir fisherman. Further large savings may be made by purchasing your rod in kit-form.

Assembling tackle

Details and diagrams will be contained in the box supplied with the fly line for fitting the backing to your reel and for joining the fly line to the backing.

Remember: a DT line may be joined to the backing at either end but a WF line may *only* be joined to the backing at the end of the thin running line. Make sure that you assemble your backing and line to the reel to suit either left or right wind. Nylon backing for a shooting head should have a string cushion wound round the reel spool, as 75 yards of heavy nylon can stress a reel to buckling point if wound on wet and tight and left to dry.

Assemble the rod by sliding the ferrules together so that all rings are dead in line (some ferrules have marks, and when these are opposite each other the rings are automatically in alignment). To get the rings in line hold the ferrules and twist slowly. Never twist the cane or glass sections of the rod, always the ferrules. Fit the reel to the reel seat and tighten the securing rings over. Make sure that the reel is correctly positioned for left or right hand wind, whichever you prefer. Guide the fly line through the line guard and pull about 12″ free. Hold the rod vertical with the handle stop on the ground and gradually 'climb up it', threading the fly line through each ring starting with the ring nearest the butt and then carefully out of the tip ring. You pull the line gently against the reel check while threading through the rings. It is very easy to miss out a ring when threading line through, particularly if you try to do it in a hurry, and if this happens you must start all over again. If there is a heavy wind blowing lean the rod with the ferrule against a firm base in such a way that the wind blows the rod towards the base and not vice versa. Next join the line to the leader and tie on a fly as described in chapter 4. Some rods are fitted with a 'keeper ring', hinged just above the butt for holding the point fly when carrying the rod. The point fly is the one tied to the far end of the leader. If there is no keeper ring then hook the point fly through the ring nearest the butt or to the reel securing ring and wind up the fly line until line and leader are tight for carrying. Do not stick the fly into the rod handle, or you will break little bits of cork out and spoilt it. If

Photographs 9–12. THE FOUR
MAJOR GROUPS

These photographs are reproduced
from *Trout Flies of Stillwater* by
kind permission of John Goddard.
They show the groups of insects
which are of particular interest to
the reservoir trout.

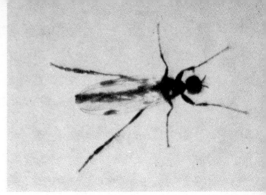

Flat-winged fly – Diptera

Fly with roof-shaped wings –
Trichoptera

Upwinged fly – Ephemeroptera

Hard-winged fly – Plecoptera

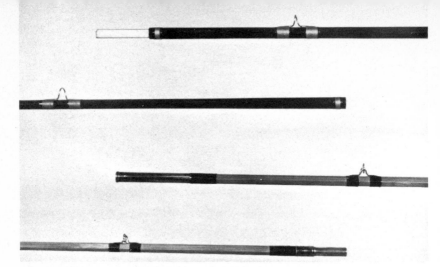

Photograph 13. Different ferrules on hollow glass and built cane rods. The hollow glass rod is fitted with a modern spigot ferrule and the cane rod has the traditional metal ferrule. The male and female sections are reversed in design. The butt of each rod would be to the right of this photograph. The hollow glass rod is fitted with snake rings and this cane rod has full open bridge rings. Cane rods are frequently fitted with snake rings also.

Photograph 14. A traditional 3½" diameter fly reel with line guard from Farlow's Serpent range. It will hold a 30-yard A F T M 6 line plus 75 yards of backing. The Air Cel Supreme is a high quality floating line and as with any other good fly line full details for assembly and maintenance are included in the line package.

Below: Photograph 15. Handles and reel seats of a hollow glass (far left) and a built cane rod. Both have firm screw-type reel fittings and each handle is made from high quality cork sections shaped and bonded. The hollow glass rod is from the Gold Band series and the built cane rod is a Sharpe's Scottie; both are manufactured by Messrs C Farlow and Co. Ltd.

Right: Photograph 16. An enlargement of A F T M markings on a 9' 0" Hardy Jet hollow glass rod and a 9' 6" Sharpe's Scottie built cane rod. The left hand marking indicates that the rod should be matched by an A F T M 6 line and for the cane rod an A F T M 7 line is required. A rod must be matched by the correct *weight* of line, and the A F T M classifications are described in chapter 3.

you have waded into the water and want to change a fly or leader without getting back to the bank, stuff the rod butt and reel well into the top of one wader. This will leave the rod upright and you will have both hands free.

Carrying tackle

It helps to keep certain things in certain pockets because in this way you can have a spot check before leaving the car, and if you adopt a system you know where things are when it gets dark. Any system will do and as an example mine works like this:

Fishing jacket breast pocket	Fishing permit, leader box and spare leaders.
Fishing jacket left hand pocket	Spare reel with alternate line, small torch, polaroid glasses.
Fishing jacket right hand pocket	Priest and clean rag. Plastic bags for fish.
Waist bag	Three boxes or tins for lures and wet flies, nymphs and dry flies. Scissors secured to belt by lanyard. Silicone dressing. Large safety pin for cleaning fly eyes. Tin of Mucilin. Detergent pad.

In spite of all these bits and pieces there is still plenty of room for a couple of apples or a bar of chocolate thanks to the ingenuity of the jacket manufacturer. I always keep my car keys in a deep trouser pocket and usually with a large safety pin through the trouser and key ring. Once you have dropped your keys in a weed bed at dusk you will soon learn to do something like this. Photograph 33 facing page 80 shows me with my favourite tackle and photograph 35 facing page 81 shows the contents of my waist bag and jacket pockets.

FISHING BAG: If I am off for the day I take a small bag for food and drink and I like to have the trout spoon and magnifier for a bit of research. We shall see later how it pays to spend a while searching for signs of insect life and other small creatures which are eaten by the trout.

LANDING NET: I always wear mine slung, and fold the deep net over the net frame when wandering around so that it does not get caught up in brambles, reeds, thistles and so on.

ROD: As a general rule always carry your rod with the butt and reel forward. If you stumble the butt will probably take the shock and there is less chance of damaging the rod tip. But sometimes it is better to carry the rod with the tip leading forward, particularly if you are passing through thickly wooded parts, because in this way you can guide the tip carefully first.

Care of tackle

ROD: After fishing wipe down your rod with a clean dry rag and put it away in the rod bag. Make sure you wipe the rings and put the end stopper into the female ferrule and always keep the rod joints clean. Do not oil metal ferrules as grit will accumulate—it is better to wipe the male ferrule on your nose as there is sufficient of nature's grease there to ease fitting. Never leave rod sections in a container tube for long and keep your rod hanging up in a dry rod bag in a dry, well-ventilated cupboard or store. Do not lie the rod down on the bank when resting—if you don't tread on it, it is quite possible that someone else will. It is better to make some sort of a rest for the rod ferrule to lean on so that the rod is clearly visible above the bank foliage, and if a strong wind is blowing secure the rod to the improvised rest with a piece of rag.

REEL: Clean and oil at the beginning and end of the season. Wipe it free from grit or mud and dry it carefully if soaking wet. Strip off wet nylon backing if the reel is to remain unused for a while to avoid the stressing which will be caused by nylon drying out.

FLY LINE: It is very important to avoid damage to the plastic coating. Do not tread on it or pinch it in the reel. Do not pull knots out if they occur after a piece of reed or twig has got mixed up in coils. Never bend the fly line back on itself. Follow the instructions supplied with the new line for maintenance. Wipe your line down with clean rag after a day's fishing to remove the scum which often occurs during warm weather. Although plastic coated lines can be left on their reels without harm it pays to strip off line after fishing and leave it in large coils on a clean flat surface.

WADERS: Do not leave them in the boot of the car to 'sweat'. Never dry them out quickly by a fire or boiler. Hang them up by the feet, and if they are saturated, fill them with dry newspaper so that they gradually dry out. It is easy to make a boot holder out of bent wire or rope so that they are supported by the feet and hang down.

NYLON AND LEADERS: Check and renew your nylon spools each season as required. Nylon loses strength with age so do not keep leaders for too long. Renew leader points frequently and check the knots. Remove little strands of weed which become tangled around the leader knots. If you ever see a tackle shop with nylon spools or made-up leaders in the window where the sun streams in, do not buy a thing in the place because the shopkeeper hasn't a clue. One of the first things to understand about nylon monofilament is that it tends to deteriorate if left exposed to sunshine or bright light for a long period.

FLIES: Discard any which show signs of rust. Check the barbs constantly and sharpen the hook points with a fine stone. A sharp hook point ought to make a score if you draw it across your thumb nail.

Further advice about tackle

DIY: The 'do it yourself' man can put his skill to good effect in the field of fishing tackle. He can buy all the materials and parts required for rod building and save a great deal of expense. He can learn to tie his own flies, tie up leaders, make a landing net and concoct all kinds of shooting heads by using parts of old fly lines for this purpose. There are a number of evening classes run during winter months covering tackle, fly tying and reservoir fishing methods as a whole and you can usually find details of these in either of the fishing journals mentioned in Appendix A.

INSURANCE: For a very modest premium it is possible to insure all your tackle against loss or damage while fishing and obtain valuable cover against personal accidents or damage to others. It is very well worth while getting a proposal form from one of the principal insurance companies because accidents can—and frequently do—happen in this game just as in other forms of sport.

'THE TRUTH ABOUT TACKLE': This is the title of a first-class comprehensive booklet written by Dermot Wilson, an exceptionally experienced fly fisherman in business at his home at Nether Wallop Mill, Stockbridge, Hampshire. It is very well illustrated and provides 74 questions with detailed answers on every aspect of tackle design. It is the best guide to trout fly tackle I have ever read, and a beginner should obtain a copy as soon as possible.

4

Getting Tied Up

This chapter deals with some of the popular knots used by reservoir fishermen and their application to leaders, fly lines and flies.

Leaders

Just as it is essential to match your rod with the correct weight of line, it pays equally well to take care with the type of leader between fly line and fly, or flies if more than one is to be used.

A leader should be tied so that it decreases in diameter from the 'butt', i.e. the thick part at which it is joined to the fly line, down to the fine end which is called the 'point'. The length of a leader varies to suit different styles of reservoir fishing. Some fishermen use leaders of 15′ 0″ and more in length but for a beginner a useful length under normal fishing conditions should be about 9′ 0″, and as he improves this may be increased to about 12′ 0″. The object of having a longish leader is to keep as great a distance as possible between the end of the fly line and the fly itself, thus giving a better margin for deceiving a fish who may well be scared off by what to him looks like an anchor cable above his window but which is in fact the tip of the fly line. However, as an exception to the general rule regarding longish leaders, it pays to use a stoutly tied leader no more than about 7′ 6″ in length when casting against a heavy wind for trout grubbing around in the surf which is driven towards you under these conditions. A long leader would be quite unmanageable in this situation. A well tied leader must be thought of as an extension to the tip of the fly line. It follows that the diameter of the butt end wants to be just a little under the diameter of the fly line tip.

The breaking strain of the point will probably be governed by the reservoir regulations but very fine points are admirable for deceiving fish under bright and sunny conditions. If the choice is left to the discretion of the fisherman then he will sometimes select as fine a point as he dare having regard to the probable size and weight of the fish available in any particular reservoir.

There are endless combinations of leader tyings but here is an example of one to give a 9' 0" leader where the reservoir regulations stipulate that a minimum breaking strain of 6 lb is acceptable:

Length of nylon	Diameter (mm)	B S (lb)
48"	·35	12¼
21"	·30	9½
18"	·26	7
21"	·24	6¼

108" = 9' 0" leader with 6¼ lb B S point.

Here is another where 4 lb B S is acceptable at the point:

Length of nylon	Diameter (mm)	B S (lb)
48"	·35	12¼
15"	·30	9½
12"	·26	7
12"	·22	5¼
21"	·20	4

108" = 9' 0" leader with 4 lb B S point.

For fishing into rough water against adverse winds—probably with a heavy fly—a shorter leader of about 7' 6" is useful and could be prepared on these lines:

Length of nylon	Diameter (mm)	B S (lb)
26"	·40	16½
24"	·35	12¼
22"	·30	9½
18"	·26	7

90" = 7' 6" leader with 7 lb B S point.

When you become proficient at presenting your fly neatly with a 9' 0" leader, extend the leader butt by a further foot and add two feet to the point so as to give at 12' 0" leader.

Some fishermen like the butt of a leader to contain a loop to which the fly line is attached. Others prefer the tip of the fly line to be extended by a section of nylon about 3' 0" in length and about two-thirds the diameter of the fly line tip, and the leader is then attached to this extension. The advantage of this method is that when the fly line is retrieved there is very little, if any, 'wake' caused by the fly line tip, whereas when there is a knot between the line tip and leader loop, wake is not so easy to avoid. The problem of wake does not become important when fishing a sunk line, but for more delicate tactics it is very important indeed. There is the further point that the additional 3' 0" or so of nylon extension makes a valuable increase in leader length.

Knots

These are so much better demonstrated than written about, but it is a good idea to learn the basic knots which have been developed for use with nylon monofilament by practising with lengths of plastic-coated clothes line or supple flex as used by electricians. Photographs 17 to 31, between pages 64 and 65 show various stages in tying the knots described in this section. The captions give further information and instruction about each knot. Once you get the various turns firmly in mind, change from flex to thick nylon and then finish up with the same routine using the finer diameters.

In the knot-tying photographs the 'fly eye' has been made from mild steel rod chemically blackened and the 'nylon' and 'fly line' are of plastic coated electrical flex. The knots which are most frequently required may be summarized as follows:

BLOOD BIGHT LOOP: For making a loop at the butt of a leader.

BLOOD KNOT: For joining two lengths of nylon.

BLOOD KNOT WITH A DROPPER LINK: For joining two lengths of nylon in such a way that a dropper fly may be added to the leader if required.

'PLATIL' KNOT: An alternative knot for joining two lengths of nylon as recommended by the manufacturers of Platil monofilament.

TUCKED HALF BLOOD KNOT: For joining nylon to the eye of a fly.

TURLE KNOT: An alternative knot for joining nylon to the eye of

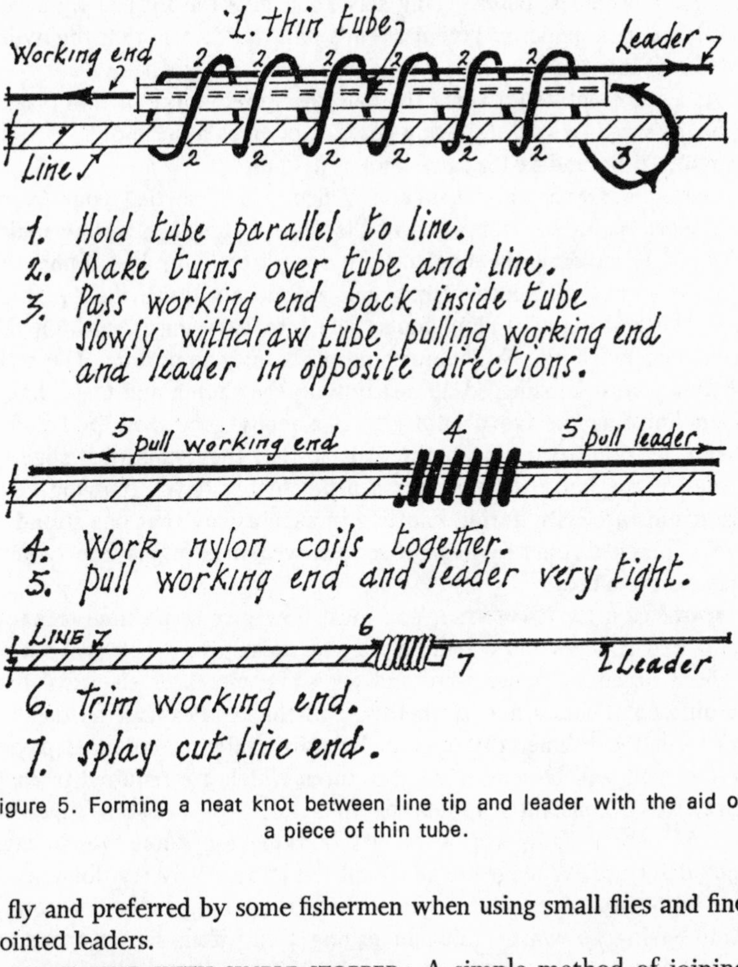
1. thin tube
Working end
Leader
2 2 2 2 2 2
Line
2 2 2 2 2 2 3
1. Hold tube parallel to line.
2. Make turns over tube and line.
3. Pass working end back inside tube
Slowly withdraw tube pulling working end
and leader in opposite directions.
5 pull working end
4
5 pull leader
4. Work nylon coils together.
5. pull working end and leader very tight.
LINE
6
7
Leader
6. trim working end.
7. splay cut line end.

Figure 5. Forming a neat knot between line tip and leader with the aid of a piece of thin tube.

a fly and preferred by some fishermen when using small flies and fine pointed leaders.

SHEET BEND WITH SIMPLE STOPPER: A simple method of joining the tip of the fly line to a blood bight loop at the butt of a leader.

NAIL KNOT: For joining a length of nylon to the fly line. This knot takes a bit of practice but once mastered is a very valuable member of the nylon knot family. The nail is laid parallel to the fly line tip and held firm. The nylon is wound as indicated and then pushed back through the space left as the nail is gradually withdrawn. The two ends of nylon are pulled in opposite directions and the nylon coils gradually bite into the line. The tighter the nylon is pulled, the tighter the knot becomes. Before tying this knot, give the fly line tip a rub with fine glass paper to give it a 'cat's paw' surface so that the nylon bites well into the line core.

As an alternative for tying the nail knot, use a piece of thin plastic tube, as supplied with fly tying gear, or perhaps a piece of 1½" long thin Biro tube, and tie the same knot as in figure 5.

FINISHING KNOTS AND LEADERS: When you have tied your fly to the leader point or dropper, give the knot a thorough testing under tension by holding the hook and nylon directly in line. Mind the hook does not stick into your finger, and do not crush the fly dressing. The making of nylon knots falls into two stages, making the turns and finishing off. The finishing off is most important. The coils of nylon must be snugged up neatly with the thumb and finger nails. After finishing the blood knot give it a really good slow pull under steady tension, then cut off the ends so that they stand just slightly proud of the knot, to allow for a little further 'give'. If nylon coils are made carelessly during knotting in such a way that one strand is badly 'pinched', there will be a serious weakness in the knot which may lead to a break.

KNOT-TYING EXPERIMENTS: You must now give some time to knotting-tying experiments and it will help if you make up a 'hook eye' out of a piece of heavy gauge wire and get some pieces of electrical flex of different colours and diameters. The thicker flex can be the 'fly line' and the thinner the 'nylon'. By using different coloured pieces of flex you will be able to see the turns which are required in each knot. Refer constantly to photographs 17 to 31 between pages 64 and 65, which show various stages in tying the knots which have been described. When you can tie all the knots easily try doing each one with your eyes shut because there is nothing more frustrating than having to waste valuable fishing time after sunset spending longer than need be when tying on a fresh fly or when making a quick change in a leader.

After some practice you will soon get the necessary turns in mind and then will be the time to put away the flex and other experimental gear and continue the good work as previously recommended, starting with thick nylon and eventually finishing with the finer diameters.

A SIMPLE LEADER-MAKING OUTFIT: Figure 6 shows a simple outfit I use. It consists of a piece of 2" × 1" prepared deal about 2' 6" long and has a stout nail driven up through the centre. It is marked off in

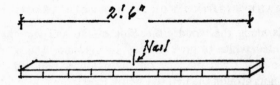

2'6"

Nail

2"x1" deal batten with 3" divisions

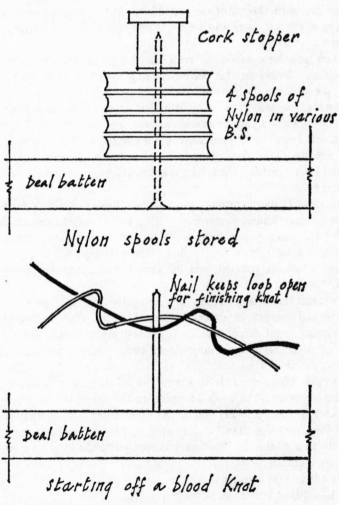

Cork stopper

4 spools of
Nylon in various
B.S.

Deal batten

Nylon spools stored

Nail keeps loop open
for finishing knot

Deal batten

starting off a blood knot

Figure 6. A leader-making outfit.

3" intervals along the wood either side of the nail and the central part is painted white to give an easy background. The 3" divisions are there so that I can measure off the nylon as required. By tying the blood knots around the nail the centre loop is kept open, and when not in use the nylon spools can sit one on top of the other with the nail passing through the centre of each. A stout cork makes a safe capping for the nail head. I usually tie up about half a dozen leaders at one go, with the outfit on a window sill to get good light, then put the whole lot away so that the nylon spools are not left exposed to light or sunshine.

When you have made up each leader give it a really thorough stretching. Always do this before starting to fish as well, because it helps the leader to straighten out on the water.

DISPOSAL OF WASTE NYLON: Whether at home or on a reservoir bank, keep waste nylon in an old envelope and burn it. Any length of nylon left lying about can cause untold suffering if a bird or other wild creature gets tangled up. Cut any disused leaders into short lengths before putting them in the old envelope, otherwise they tend to spring out.

CHECKING LEADERS DURING USE: When fishing, make a frequent check of your leader. Remove any little bits of weed or scum from the knots. When you change a fly, nip off an inch from the point and tie your new fly to fresh nylon. After playing a fish always have a careful look at your fly and fly knot before continuing the good work.

KNOTLESS LEADERS: These are available through good tackle dealers and consist of extended monofilament with a continuous diminishing taper from butt to tip. They are excellent for fishing amongst weed because the absence of knots makes a perfectly clean retrieve possible.

A NYLON 'COLLAR': This is a most useful device. It is formed by joining about 2' 0" of 20 lb BS nylon to the tip of the fly line by a nail knot or needle splice, and at the other end I form a small blood bight loop, no more than ¼" diameter, tightened very hard to reduce its bulk to a minimum. The leader is secured to the loop by a tucked half blood knot.

The advantages here are:
1. Changes of leader can be made quickly.
2. The loop at the end of the nylon extension is very handy for

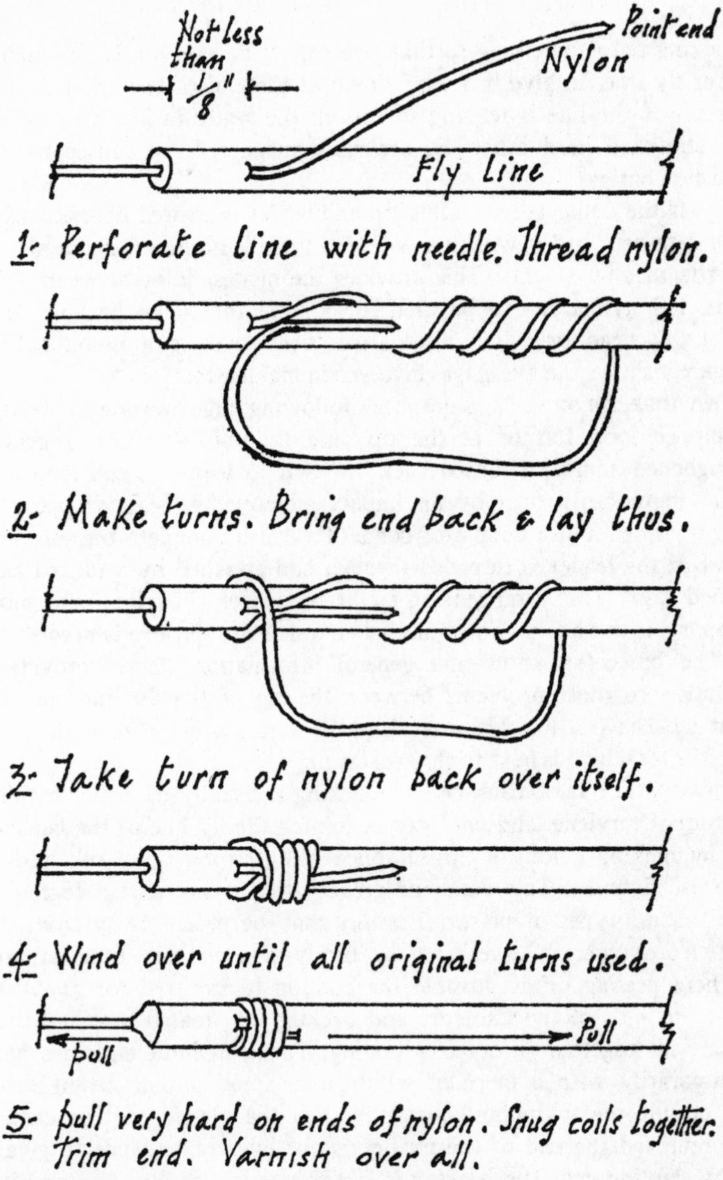

Not less than 1/8"

Point end

Nylon

Fly Line

1- Perforate line with needle. Thread nylon.

2- Make turns. Bring end back & lay thus.

3- Take turn of nylon back over itself.

4- Wind over until all original turns used.

pull

Pull

5- pull very hard on ends of nylon. Snug coils together. Trim end. Varnish over all.

Figure 7. Five stages in making a needle splice. This very neat joint can be used between line tip and leader or for joining nylon backing to a shooting head.

hooking onto something so that you can walk backwards unwinding your fly line, to give it a wipe down at the end of fishing or a mild stretch if the line is tending to coil on the water (a line must *never* be stretched hard otherwise serious damage will be caused to the plastic coating).

3. If the collar between line tip and leader is treated liberally with the detergent pad it will sink well and there is no line wake at all.

THE NEEDLE SPLICE: This provides the neatest joint between a fly line and nylon. It can be used for joining the nylon backing to a shooting head or as an alternative when making a nylon collar. Figure 7 shows the five stages involved in making this joint.

A WHIPPED LOOP: Photograph 28 following page 64 shows a neatly-whipped loop formed at the tip of a fly line. The line is gently roughened and then turned back on itself to form a small loop and held temporarily firm by an impact adhesive. A neat whipping is then formed and a couple of coats of varnish complete the job. The butt of the leader is threaded through and attached by a tucked half blood knot. This arrangement facilitates leader changing—and most important there is no line wake when a delicate retrieve is needed.

The preceding knots and general information should provide a solution to most problems between the tip of the fly line and fly, but let's have a look at what happens at the other end of the line, i.e. the bit which is next to the reel drum.

JOINING FLY LINE TO BACKING: Backing is usually of heavy braided rot-proof terylene, and one way of joining the fly line to the backing is by making a long whipped splice using strong tying silk with a varnished finish. This demands great patience and a fair degree of skill. Some types of plastic dressings may be peeled away from the line core whereas others are so firmly bonded that they cannot. Where peeling off is possible the coating is removed for about 2" and the ends of the line core and backing are 'teased out' and then 'married' together prior to whipping. The teased-out ends are held temporarily with a piece of sellotape or some similar arrangement to permit the whipping to start. When the plastic coating cannot be removed the end of the fly line is cut by a razor blade to give a long slanting end. The backing is laid to overlap the line and slanting end and a whipped finish made as before. It helps if some impact adhesive is applied to join the two before starting the whipping. An alternative method of joining backing to the fly line is to form at the start of the fly line a whipped loop through which the backing is secured by a tightly drawn tucked half blood knot. It is most important to check that the joint between fly line and backing will pass freely out *and back* through the top ring of the rod tip. A neat long whipped splice always will and the alternative usually will, but it is worth checking because if a strong fish makes several long runs during which line and backing are extended there may be a break and a lost fish if the joint between line and backing cannot travel smoothly through the rod rings.

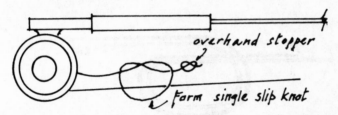

Figure 8. A simple knot for joining terylene backing to the reel spool.

Joining backing to spool

When terylene backing is used figure 8 shows a method suitable for this job. The stopper at the spare end of the slip knot is an additional safety measure. When winding on backing, make sure it is placed very evenly in the drum—not too tight and certainly not loose. When winding the fly line on take great care to get it evenly distributed nice and firmly, and avoid loose overlaps. Above all make sure you are winding in the right direction to suit your requirements for either left or right hand wind. Some fishermen prefer using strong nylon, about 20 lb BS, as backing. If this is used it can be joined to the reel spool by forming a 'noose'. This is easily done by first tying a blood bight loop at the end of the backing and then passing the backing through the loop and thus making an extra secure slip knot over the spool. Where nylon backing is used it can be joined to the fly line by a needle splice or nail knot. Alternatively form a whipped loop at the start of the fly line and join the nylon backing to the loop with a tucked half blood knot.

Joining backing to shooting head

In this case the backing will most probably be nylon of about

25–30 lb B S. If it is a newly purchased shooting head there is almost certain to be a loop at the back end. The nylon may be fixed to this loop with a tucked half blood knot. If you have made up a shooting head from an old length of fly line then join the nylon backing to the shooting head with a neatly made needle splice. This should travel freely through the top rod ring. The forward tip of a shooting head may be joined to the leader by any of the methods previously outlined as for standard fly line to leader joints.

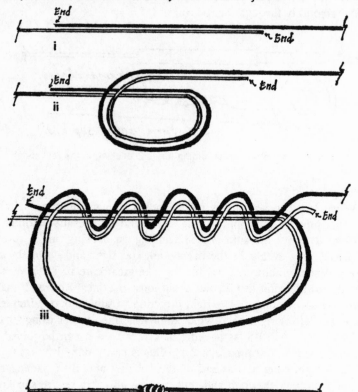

Figure 8a. The four-turn water knot is a very useful alternative for joining two lengths of nylon, as shown. The lengths are first held parallel so as to overlap about 4" or so, then both are turned into a loop as in ii. The four turns are completed as in iii (enlarged) and then the knot is drawn tight, after which the ends are trimmed off. It is important to work the turns evenly as the knot is drawn together and to leave about $\frac{1}{16}$" of each trimmed end to allow for a little 'give'. This knot is suitable for joining the finer strands of nylon up to about 9 lb B S but above this size the blood knot should be used as it is less bulky.

5

Elementary Casting and Line Control

Learning to cast a fly line is not difficult, and this chapter explains the basic movements which will help the beginner to cast a neat and accurate line up to twenty yards or so. Long distance casting into the forty-yard range calls for specialized tackle and a casting style known as the 'double haul', and this type of casting is not within the scope of this book—neither can it be learnt correctly without first mastering the principles of simple casting. Without wishing to repeat too often what has been written before I want to emphasize that it is not necessary to become a long distance caster to catch trout from the banks of reservoirs provided you are prepared to avoid the more popular areas and adopt exploratory tactics at the less fished parts.

The guidance in this chapter is written for the right-handed fisherman. If you hold your rod with the left hand then please read 'right' for 'left' and vice versa.

Before running through the principles of casting I would like you to follow a simple experiment. In order to carry it out you need your rod, reel, line and a 9′ leader suitably assembled, and in addition a piece of string about ten feet long—and a ladder. Lean the ladder close to a rain water pipe or perhaps a soil stack at the back of your house, climb up and tie the piece of string firmly to the pipe not less than fifteen feet above the ground. Now fasten the other end of the string to the leader by making a blood bight loop at the leader point, thread the string through and tighten up with a simple slip knot. Pay out about ten feet of line beyond the tip of your rod, hold the rod upright and walk gradually away from the pipe to which the string, leader and line are now attached. The neighbours will think you have gone quite mad but there's more to come yet.

When you are far enough away, tighten the line from rod tip to pipe, hold the butt of the rod vertical and the set-up ought to look as in figure 9. Note particularly that the line, leader and string are not parallel to the ground but inclined at a slight angle *upwards* from the horizontal. An an alternative to tying the string to a pipe it may be possible to secure it to an upstairs window catch. It doesn't matter what you fix it to but it must be at least fifteen feet up from ground level. If you live in a bungalow then you must find a piece of open ground with a tree on it and tie the string to a branch at the same height.

Your rod is nine feet long and you should hold it firmly with the thumb and fingers as in figure 10, with the reel pointing dead ahead about five feet above ground level. Squeeze the rod handle and *keeping the butt of the rod completely vertical* push your rod so that the butt and reel move forward about twelve inches in a horizontal plane. Do not twist your wrist sideways but do push the butt with your thumb. This movement should not result in a well-maintained pipe coming away from the wall but it ought to produce a very promi-

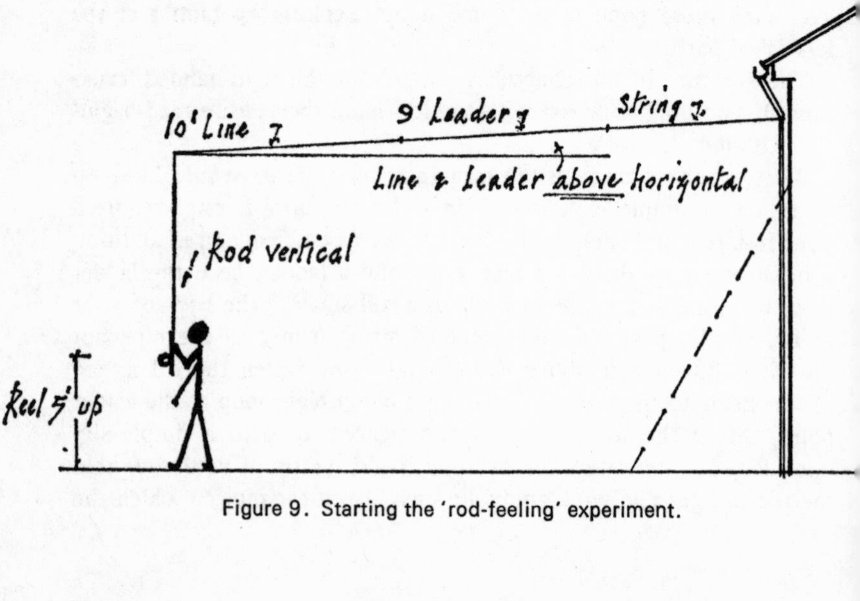

Figure 9. Starting the 'rod-feeling' experiment.

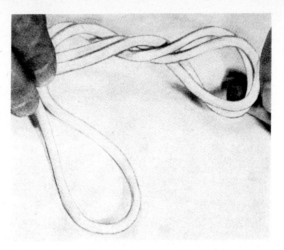

Photographs 17–20. Start a blood bight loop by doubling the nylon back on itself, and form two twists between the single and double loops.

Maintain the twists and pass the single loop through the *back* of the double loop.

Work the turns evenly and draw them together.

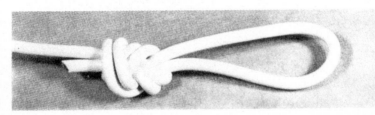

Pull very tight, snug the coils of nylon neatly and trim off the spare end. The blood bight loop cannot slip, and is used when a loop is required at the butt end of a leader or as part of a nylon 'collar', the purpose of which is described in chapter 4.

Photographs 21–22. The blood knot is used for joining two lengths of nylon Make four turns of the thinner strand and three of the thicker. By using the outfit shown in figure 6 on page 57, the centre loop of the blood knot is kept open. When tying this knot at the waterside a matchstick, pin or reed stem can be used for the same purpose.

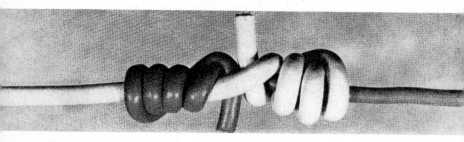

When finishing off the blood knot work the coils neatly together and pull very tight. Trim off the ends but leave about $\frac{1}{16}$" of each end projecting to allow for a little 'give'.

Photograph 23. A blood knot with a dropper link. Dropper links are needed in leaders when more than one fly is to be tied on. Links can be left when tying the blood knots which join each section of nylon, and if the thicker strand of nylon is left as the link the dropper fly will stand clear and have less tendency to tangle. The dropper link runs off the bottom of this photograph.

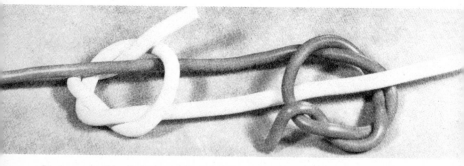

Photograph 24. An alternative method of joining two lengths of nylon as recommended by the manufacturers of Platil. It is easier to tie than the blood knot. The turns of each are worked closely together and snugged into each other as the two knots are pulled firmly together. Trim off the surplus ends and leave about $\frac{1}{16}$" proud as recommended for the blood knot.

Photograph 25. A tucked half blood knot is simple and reliable for tying nylon to the eye of a fly. The turns must be pulled up very tight to the hook eye.

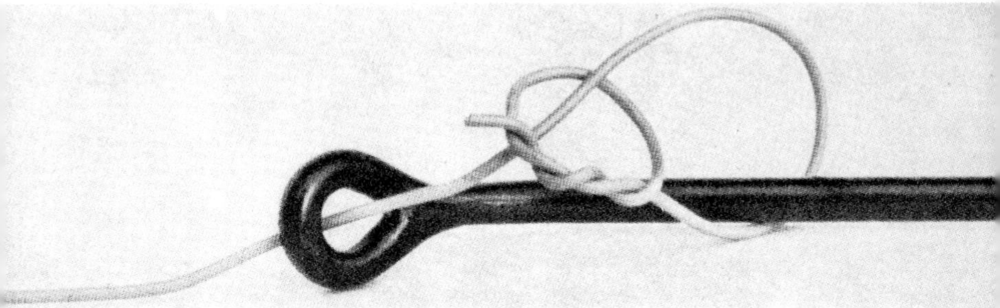

Photograph 26. A turle knot is an alternative for tying nylon to the hook eye. It is sometimes preferable when tying small flies to finely pointed leaders.

Photograph 27. A simple method of joining the tip of the fly line to a leader. Firstly tie an overhead knot, pulled tight at the tip of the fly line. Then pass the line tip through the blood bight loop at the butt of the leader and form a single bend as indicated. Both line and leader will become firmly jammed by drawing tight. The disadvantage of this joint is its relative bulk which creates 'wake' during a slow retrieve in calm water.

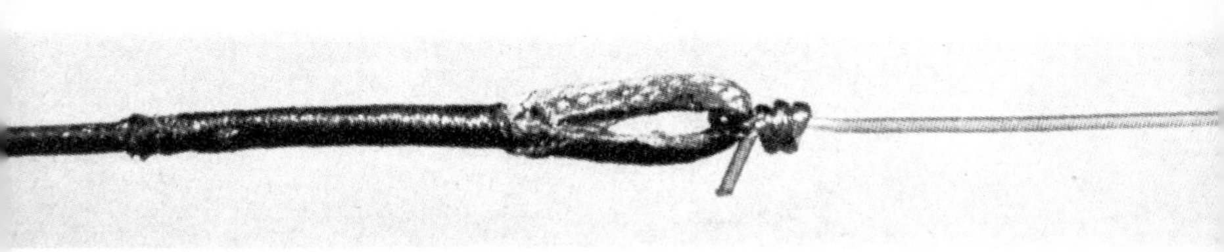

Photograph 28. An enlargement of a whipped loop formed at the tip of a fly line with the butt of a leader secured by a tucked half blood knot. A small loop at the tip of the fly line makes leader changing very simple and there is no bulk to create 'wake' during a slow retrieve. The same joint may be used for joining nylon backing to the back end of a shooting head.

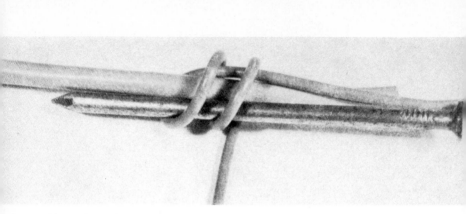

Photographs 29–31. To start a nail knot hold the nail parallel to the fly line tip and make two turns with the working end. These turns go over the nail, fly line and standing end of the nylon. In this example the working end is pointing down and the leader will be a continuation of the nylon to the right of the nail head.

Make two or three further complete turns and tuck the working end back through the space between the nail and fly line. In this photograph the working end has been tucked through and is pointing in the same direction as the point of the nail.

Gradually withdraw the nail and at the same time pull the working and standing ends of the nylon in opposite directions. The harder you pull the tighter the knot will become and when finished the coils should be evenly snugged together. By pulling really hard you will make the nylon bite into the line core. Trim off the working end and splay cut the line tip. There is no bulk to this knot and it forms a good joint between line tip and leader when delicate retrieving is required.

nent curve in the rod as in figure 11. Now return the rod butt to its
original position and you will see that the rod tip straightens back
to the vertical. What has this achieved? For the first time you are
getting the *feel* of your rod as a recoil spring. Keep the butt vertical
and move it horizontally forwards and backwards in a horizontal

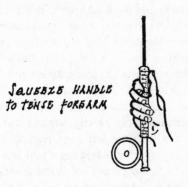

SQUEEZE HANDLE
TO TENSE FOREARM

ROD GRIP

Figure 10. By adopting this grip you are able to get the 'feel' of your rod.

plane so that you feel the power of the rod. As you push it forward
apply pressure to the butt with the ball of your thumb. Make the
rod really flex—give it some stick with this set of horizontal movements and you will feel the *action* of the rod right through from
tip to butt.

It is possible that your flexings will cause line to come off the reel.
If this happens, pinch the line with your forefinger against the butt
so that the length of line, leader and string remains constant the
whole time. Now look over your rod arm shoulder, and you will see
that when the rod is flexed the line and leader are dead straight and
pointing up from the horizontal and here is the main point of the
whole exercise; by seeing that the line and leader are straight and
inclined upwards we have achieved exactly the situation which is
needed for making a correct back cast.

By why bother about the back cast? Surely when fishing, the fly
has to go forward and we want a good forward cast? Absolutely
correct, but it is impossible to make a good forward cast unless it is

preceded by a good back cast, and once you have learnt how to make a good back cast the rest is easy.

Now resume the routine—keep the ten feet of fly line beyond the rod tip and again stand with the rod butt absolutely vertical and the line just taut between rod tip and pipe. Pull off about four feet of line from the rod with your left hand and hold it tight, down by your left-hand trouser pocket. Make a 12″ push forward with the rod butt to flex the rod as before and the set-up should now look like that in figure 12. Now, keep the same hold on the butt of the rod and still holding the line tight in your left hand raise the left hand about 16″. Watch the tip of your rod: it has straightened and the line has *sagged* as in figure 13. Now pull the line down to your left trouser pocket and you will see that the rod has flexed and the line is *tight*.

Follow this experiment very closely, always starting with a flexed rod and tight line and with the left hand holding line down by your trouser pocket. Raise left hand – feel sag – pull left hand down – feel flex – raise left hand – feel sag – pull left hand down – feel flex. Now a series of even movements. Left hand up – sag – pull – flex – up – sag – pull – flex – up – sag – pull – flex. Keep this going and look over your rod shoulder to see how the line responds to the action of the *left* hand. From this part of the experiment we have learnt another essential element in casting, namely the value of left-hand pull for keeping a taut

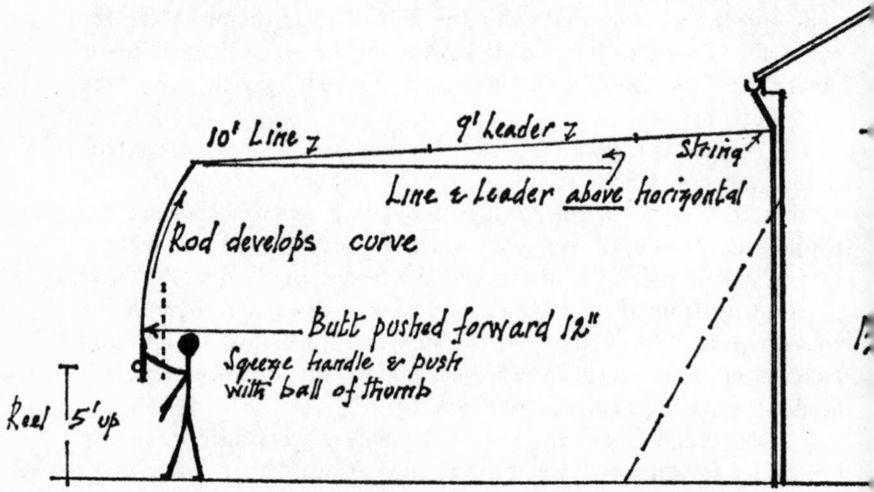

Figure 11. By flexing the rod you are able to feel its 'action'.

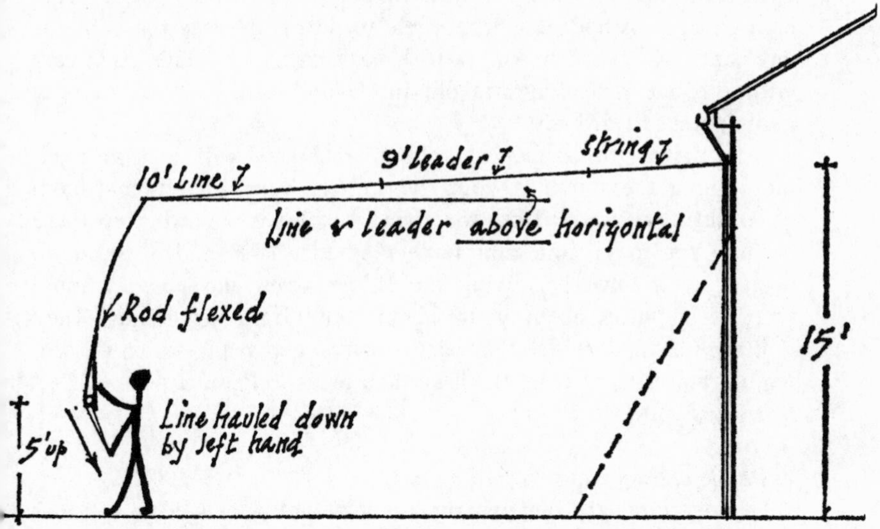

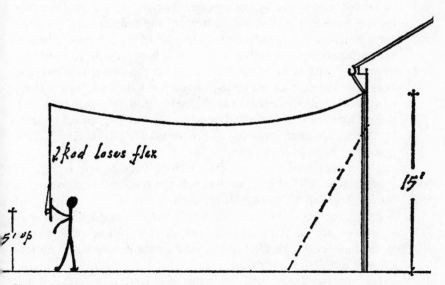

Figure 12. Left hand haul keeps a taut line and an *upward* back cast.

Figure 13. Without left hand haul the line droops and you cannot cast it forward correctly.

back cast. This pull is termed 'haul' and provides the basis of the single haul casting method. It is impossible to over-emphasize the value of left hand haul when making a high back cast, and a high back cast with the line extending straight out behind will lead you in to a really good forward cast.

Keep playing this game for an hour or so: you will learn so much more about the action of your rod and the value of left-hand haul. Then untie the leader from the string, but leave the string up there because you may want some further practice later, and if you undo it, it may involve borrowing the ladder again and possibly more worried enquiries about your mental state from neighbours. They will soon have to realize that once a person gets really set on fly fishing, normal behaviour by the fisherman tends to lapse at peak periods of enthusiasm.

A simple casting sequence

Having completed our experiments it would be as well to consider a little of the mechanics and theory of fly line casting, because there are some important principles involved and once learnt they will never be forgotten. In our experiments the rod's action was brought out by tension, and in casting this tension is provided by the weight of the fly line travelling behind and in front of the rod tip. The line hand plays a vital part in maintaining tension during the process of hauling.

In order to describe casting sequences it is convenient to imagine a huge clock with its face standing parallel to the caster. Whether you hold your rod in your left or right hand you must look for the clock over your right shoulder. When the rod is held fully extended with the tip forward in a horizontal position, the rod is described as being at the nine o'clock position. When dead upright—twelve o'clock and when inclined backwards say one or perhaps two o'clock. If the rod is moved briskly from eleven o'clock back to one o'clock its movement will be as in figure 14A and the resultant loop formed in the fly line will be narrow. If on the other hand the rod is moved briskly from ten o'clock to two o'clock its movement will be as in figure 14B and the resultant loop in the fly line will be much deeper. In the former case we describe the rod movement as making a narrow arc and in the latter a wide arc.

For reservoir fishing both accuracy and distance are required and we must concentrate on learning to keep the rod movements within

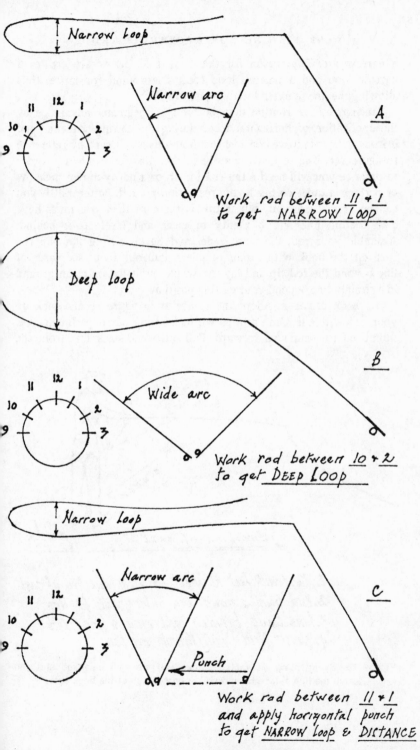

Figure 14. Some simple mechanics of fly line casting.

a narrow arc. The reason for this is that a narrow arc creates a narrow loop and a narrow loop creates less wind resistance, thus allowing the line to extend with greater distance.

The narrow arc routine may be brought to greater advantage by the application of horizontal force during the casting sequence and it is very important we consider just how this is achieved by reference to figure 14C. The sequence may be analysed as follows and in order to practice you will need a fair-sized lawn or a newly-mown meadow or perhaps a quiet corner in the recreation ground. Better still if you can be at the reservoir, but if this is the case then you must have *a* a floating line and *b* plenty of clear and level space behind. Assemble your rod, line and leader and tie on an old fly. Nip the barb off the hook with a pair of pliers. Pull out about six yards of line beyond the rod tip and lay the whole outfit flat on clean ground in a straight line beyond your casting position.

THE BACK CAST: 1. Adopt the stance as in figure 15 and pick up your rod with the same grip as we had during our experiments, i.e. thumb on top and well forward. Pull out some slack line from the

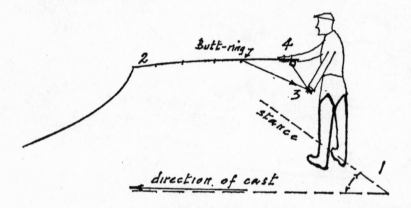

1. Stand with feet at about 45° from direction of cast
2. Rod pointed down and in line with fly line
3. Line taut between butt-ring & line hand
4. Wrist firm with thumb on top

Figure 15. By adopting an angled stance you are well balanced and can watch the line extend behind you at completion of the back cast.

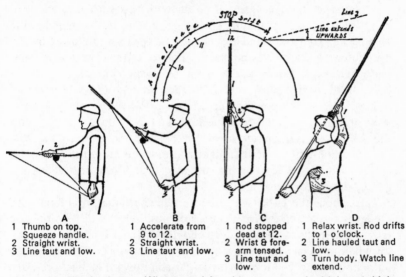

A
1 Thumb on top. Squeeze handle.
2 Straight wrist.
3 Line taut and low.

B
1 Accelerate from 9 to 12.
2 Straight wrist.
3 Line taut and low.

C
1 Rod stopped dead at 12.
2 Wrist & forearm tensed.
3 Line taut and low.

D
1 Relax wrist. Rod drifts to 1 o'clock.
2 Line hauled taut and low.
3 Turn body. Watch line extend.

Figure 16. The back cast. When practising this sequence aim high and think of it as an *upcast*. Note the essential part played by the line hand for keeping a taut line.

reel and hold this down by your left-hand trouser pocket with the line hand as photograph 36 facing page 112.

2. Squeeze the rod handle. This will tense the arm muscles.

3. Raise your rod elbow to lift the rod. Keep the wrist locked and bring the rod up very smartly with increasing speed through nine, ten and eleven o'clock, and when the rod butt gets to twelve o'clock stop the fast upward movement dead. This dead stop is achieved by tensing your forearm, wrist and hand and then immediately relaxing. At the time of the dead stop haul down hard with the line hand.

4. Bend the rod wrist and allow the rod to tip back to the one o'clock position. This tip-back is termed 'drift'.

If you have done everything right the line should fairly whizz backwards and at the peak of the back cast you should have a perfectly straight line, just as we had when the leader tip was fixed to the piece of string tied to the back of the house in our 'rod feeling' experiment. What's more, at completion of the back cast you should feel a distinct 'tug' on your flexed rod tip as the line extends.

If the whole lot falls in a heap behind you, just make a complete turn round, straighten out the leader, line and rod and take the back cast sequence through again. Keep on with this back cast and you will find it helps if you turn your head so you can watch the line unfold over your rod shoulder; making the dead stop followed by the drift to one o'clock takes much less time to do than write about and the whole back cast sequence must be crisp with the rod flexing fully, aided by line-hand haul. With each practice you will improve, and as soon as you see the line unfold for its full extent just let it drop gracefully to the ground behind you. As you get better with this back cast routine try to aim it high at the peak so that the extended line unfolds dead straight and *upwards* from the horizontal —just as it was when our line tip was fixed fifteen feet above the ground during our experiments.

Throughout the back cast sequence remember that vital haul with the left hand at the twelve o'clock stop position. It will keep the line taut as it unfolds at the rear. Keep on with this back cast sequence until the whole movement from pick-up to stop is fast and crisp with the line unfolding behind you in a dead straight and upward inclination. Have a friend standing about six yards away on the rod side so that he can congratulate you each time this essential sequence is correctly achieved.

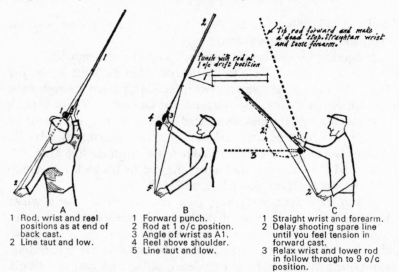

A	B	C
1 Rod, wrist and reel positions as at end of back cast. 2 Line taut and low.	1 Forward punch. 2 Rod at 1 o/c position. 3 Angle of wrist as A1. 4 Reel above shoulder. 5 Line taut and low.	1 Straight wrist and forearm. 2 Delay shooting spare line until you feel tension in forward cast. 3 Relax wrist and lower rod in follow through to 9 o/c position.

Figure 17. The forward cast and follow through. The forward punch is made with the rod at the one o'clock position. The rod is then tipped forward to the eleven o'clock position. Delay shooting spare line until you feel the tension building up as the line extends forward.

THE FORWARD CAST: This sequence will lead to a delicate and accurate delivery of the fly towards the water and if the back cast has been perfected should be comparatively easy.

1. Make your back cast exactly as described.

2. Just as the line completely unfolds at the end of the back cast and with the rod and wrist shaped as for the one o'clock position, 'punch' the rod forward, keeping the reel at the same level and maintain left hand haul as tight as possible.

It is essential to understand that this punch is the horizontal thrust imparted to the taut line and it must be started with the rod at the one o'clock drift position. It is a full arm movement by shoulder and elbow with the rod wrist remaining in the one o'clock drift position. Imagine you are pushing a weight along a shoulder-high shelf. Accelerate briskly, keep the reel above your shoulder and do not lower it.

3. Your flexed rod will now approach dead ahead and at this point, and not before, tip your rod to the eleven o'clock position by depressing your rod wrist, and again come to a dead stop by muscle tension followed by an immediate relaxation. When making the forward punch aim high by pointing the rod tip at an imaginary target well above head level.

4. As the line whips forward you will feel the tension developing in its movement and at this moment release the line which you have been holding in the haul position. This release of spare line is called 'shooting' and it is an integral part of the forward cast. By shooting line two things are achieved—*a* increased distance and *b* a delicate delivery of the fly to the water.

5. Make a gradual follow through with the rod, finally lowering the rod and casting arm to about the nine o'clock position.

To summarize our casting sequences figures 16A to 16D analyse the back cast and figures 17A to 17C the forward cast. As in any sport's action, be it an off drive at cricket, a good golf shot, or a fast service at tennis there are three basic ingredients:

1. Correct footwork
2. Timing
3. Follow through

In fly line casting, the footwork is assisted by adopting the stance recommended, so that in the early stages you can turn your head and watch the line extend backwards and upwards at completion of the back cast. Timing can only be acquired with practice but if you remember the basic movements *coupled with left-hand haul* your cast will soon be correct. The follow through is the natural conclusion at the end of the forward cast made by a graceful lowering of the rod at completion.

Remember these essential principles when practising:

1. You must not wave your rod about like a fairy's wand.

2. Always squeeze the rod handle before starting a back-cast. This will tense the arm muscles. Adopt the correct grip—as in photograph 36 facing page 112.

3. Accelerate very briskly from nine o'clock to twelve o'clock. Stop dead, apply line haul and allow the rod to drift to one o'clock by bending the rod wrist. Maintain line haul.

4. Always aim high on the back cast. Regard it more as an *up cast*. Maintain line haul.

5. Start the forward power thrust with the rod at the one o'clock position and keep it at this position for the full extent of the horizontal punch. Maintain line haul.

6. Tip the rod forward at conclusion of the punch by depressing the wrist. Push your rod thumb hard against the butt at this point and aim the tip of the rod high. Maintain line haul.

7. Once the forward tip has been completed and you feel the tension in the forward extending line, shoot the spare line from the haul position.

8. Learning to stop dead at the back cast and forward cast positions is the most important part of casting.

9. Don't get frustrated if things go wrong. Have a rest. Sort out the experiments and sequences in your mind and have another go.

10. Remember—casting a fly line is not difficult. It is strange to begin with but once you have the knack you will never forget it, just like riding a bike.

False casting

False casting is the term used for getting out sufficient length of fly line to cover the target area. In false casting the line moves back and forth in the air without touching the grass or water on the forward cast. This is to say that the back cast is started while the line is still in the air in front.

Before starting to false cast, pay out about fifteen feet of line in front of the rod and take up the same stance and rod grip as for a normal back cast. Now strip off say six yards of line from the reel and let it fall to the ground or water and remain in broad coils. Do not tread on it. Take up the left-hand haul position and make a brisk back cast from about ten to one o'clock—still with left hand haul—and aim the back cast high. Follow up with a forward cast as previously described and as the rod reaches the ten o'clock position shoot the first yard of spare line. Repeat the sequence of back and forward casting and at each forward cast shoot another yard. Do not let the forward cast drop to the grass or water, but start your back cast just after the forward shoot, and provided you maintain left-hand haul the whole time you will have a line gradually extending in length moving back and forth until you have used up all but the last two or three yards for a final shoot and delivery to the target area. When you have the whole line moving back and forth, try the following experiment.

Hook the thumb of your line-hand over the line in the haul position and keep the line hooked in this way tight to your left hand trouser pocket. Keep the same length of line moving back and forth at a steady pace and you will feel the tremendous tension which develops in the line as the rod flexes. This experiment shows again the vital part played when hauling with the line-hand. Left-hand haul means a tight line and well-flexed rod, and with these ingredients good casting must follow. This experiment will give you confidence in the flexing action of your rod, and the line-haul will make your line hand sensitive to varying degrees of line tension.

False casting should be kept to a minimum. You will find with practice that it is possible to shoot several yards of spare line in one go. This can only be achieved by keeping a high and straight back cast plus maximum rod flexing caused by strong line-hand haul. If you are using a forward taper line the rear end of the heavy belly should not be allowed more than a foot or two outside the top ring of the rod. If the thin running line is allowed out while false casting you will lose control and defeat the object for which this type of line has been designed.

Alteration of casting arc

Up to now you have been casting with the principal rod movements between eleven and one o'clock. In this way you have cast a

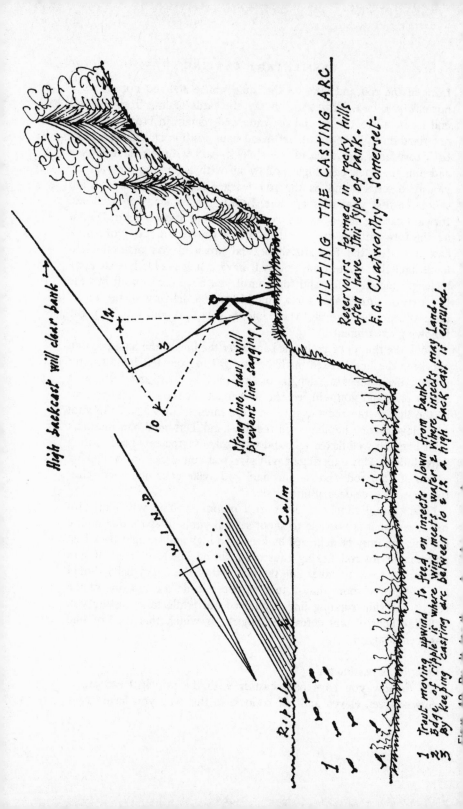

TILTING THE CASTING ARC

Reservoirs formed in rocky hills often have this type of bank. E.G. Clatworthy - Somerset.

High backcast will clear bank →

WIND

Ribble

Calm

Strong line haul will prevent line sagging

1 Trout moving upwind to feed on insects blown from bank.
2 Edge of ripple is where wind meets water & where insects may land.
3 By keeping casting arc between 10 & 1½ a high back cast if ensured.

narrow loop. In our experiments we have been lucky in not having obstacles behind so that a high and straight back cast was eventually achieved. As a beginner you must always try and find a quiet spot where such favourable conditions exist but it is not always possible. If you find yourself with a rising bank or other obstacle behind, you can still get a correct back cast by a trick known as 'tilting the arc'. This means that instead of making your rod movements between eleven and one, you make them between ten and twelve. The movements are precisely as previously described—left-hand haul is more than ever important and the end result is that you make a very much higher back cast, thus clearing the obstacle. Figure 18 shows a situation where tilting the arc is required.

Further casting instruction

The late Charles Ritz—a world class fly caster—wrote a magnificent book *A Fly Fisher's Life* (revised edition 1972, published by Reinhardt). Although it is primarily for the river fisherman you must get this book on loan from the library and read all he has to say on the different methods of casting a fly line. It is written in a most practical style and the photographs and casting illustrations are exceptionally good.

In addition you must study the excellent photographed casting sequence in T. C. Ivens' *Still Water Fly Fishing*, and for a very modest outlay of less than 50p you must buy a most instructive booklet *To Cast a Trout Fly* published by Messrs Farlow and Hardy Brothers in conjunction with Scientific Anglers Inc. of America. This book is very well illustrated, and in addition to the simple casting I have described it covers long distance work coupled with the 'double haul' style, also the 'roll cast' by which a line is picked up from the water and re-cast without any back cast at all. Also the 'side cast' which is really a horizontal application of the overhand casting style which we have examined.

Some 'dont's' when making your casting debut at the waterside

1. Don't feel embarrassed. Every fisherman has found fly line casting a bit difficult to start with. A passing angler may well come over and offer to help you out. If he does, accept warmly.

2. Don't get amongst other fishermen. You may have to walk a

long way but you must have space and quiet in which to practise.
You must also have a firm foothold.

3. Don't try with a sinking line. Unless you remember to bring all
but the last yard or two up through the water prior to making a back
cast you could break your rod. A floating line will lift off from the
water surface without any danger.

4. Don't pick a spot where it is obvious you are going to have
restricted space for your back cast.

5. Don't choose somewhere with a high wind directly behind you.
A slight cross wind is more favourable, the direction depending as
to whether you are right or left handed.

6. Don't expect to catch a fish. Your first line-thrash on the water,
which will probably occur from a mis-timed forward cast, will scare
all fish out of reasonable casting distance.

Some casting problems and suggested remedies

1. Back cast touches ground. Remedy: keep casting movements
between eleven and one o'clock and maintain left-hand haul. Watch
line extend upwards during back cast.

2. 'Wind knots' form in leader. A wind knot is formed when the
leader curls back and through itself due to mistiming of the casting
movements. Remedy: allow back cast to extend fully before starting
power punch, and make sure power punch is started with rod in the
one o'clock position.

3. Fly hooks itself around line. Remedy: as 2, allow back cast to
extend fully before starting power punch and make sure power punch
is started with rod in the one o'clock position.

4. Line and leader fall in a heap at end of forward cast. Remedy:
either delay shooting line until sufficient tension is developed in the
forward extending line, or you have been waving your rod like a
fairy queen between ten and two instead of working it hard between
eleven and one, and in either case you have not paid attention to
the esssential effect of left-hand line haul.

5. Fly snaps off or breaks hook barb. Remedy: forward cast started
too soon or back cast was allowed to drop (a common fault when
fishing from a dam face). Keep a high back cast. Maintain line-haul
and watch line unfold upwards. Memorize the term 'up cast' and
relate it to each back cast.

6. Leader and line slap water. Remedy: forward cast aimed too

low. Get into the correct casting arc and deliver the forward cast high above water. Do not lean forward at the end of forward cast.

7. Line will not go out. Remedy : you may have missed out a ring when threading line during assembly, or perhaps you have twisted the line around the rod between two rings. Or you have been waving that wand again, probably between nine and three o'clock. Get into the correct arc, work briskly and use plenty of left-hand haul to keep a tight line.

Problems in casting tend to accumulate when you are tired. When practising keep each session to about half an hour and then have a good break, during which time sit down and mentally analyse each step in the casting sequences. You will gain nothing by flogging away when things are going wrong, better by far to give it a rest and work out *why* things are going wrong. If you have a correctly balanced rod and line then casting should be quite effortless. If you find your casting means real hard physical exertion then you must stop, because you are completely out of casting form and have not devoted sufficient time to learning the proper sequence of movements.

Casting into wind

Whether you are fishing as a beginner or as an experienced fisherman, reservoirs are such that changes in wind direction can occur quite unexpectedly and often do. It usually pays to cast with a slight following wind because you can generally cover fish who tend to move into the wind—and a slight following wind behind you will make your casting easier.

If the wind suddenly veers round you have two alternatives. You can either move off to a more comfortable casting position or you must cast into it. It usually pays to stay put because if you have seen fish moving prior to the change in wind it is unlikely that they will change their ground as quickly as the wind has changed its direction. It usually takes several hours before fish alter their cruising courses following a change in wind direction.

It is under these conditions of difficult wind that the forward taper line makes such a difference; as you will remember, the weight in this line is concentrated into the first thirty feet or so and this assists in penetrating the wind during the forward cast. There is a valuable trick to be learnt for casting into wind, and again it centres on correct timing of the forward shoot. If you 'cut down' your rod parallel to the water surface *before* shooting line, you will 'get under the wind' and make a much better job of things. Remember also that under windy conditions a 7′ 6″ leader with a stout butt will serve much better than a long one which can become quite unmanageable when casting into a gusty wind.

Dangers and snags in casting

1. If you are fishing heavy lures or large flies during blustering winds take the precaution of wearing a pair of goggles.

2. It is better to fish a single fly during windy conditions because the chances of tangles are less than if fishing a leader with two or three flies.

3. Fish one fly only after dark. In this way the risks of tangles are kept to a minimum.

4. Fishing a single fly gives a better margin for success if a hooked fish decides to run into weed. If there is a dropper fly under similar conditions, and the dropper hook becomes fast in the weed, the chances of a break are considerable.

5. If you discover a wind knot in your leader, stop fishing. Take the knot apart using either a pin or the hook of another fly. If the knot comes apart easily give the leader a thorough stretch to test its strength. A single wind knot in a leader can tighten to the point of cutting the nylon. If you have any doubt about damage to the strength of the leader where the knot occurred then change the leader.

6. If you get into a tangle at night it is usually quicker to change a leader than to waste valuable time trying to sort things out. It pays to have a spare leader with your favourite evening fly tied on just in case this occurs. If tangles occur during day-time fishing it is best to take the flies off before unravelling the leader.

7. Always give very adequate clearance when passing behind another fisherman. If he is a long distance caster he may have thirty yards of line out on the back cast, plus an eighteen foot leader, so play it safe and give him or any other fisherman far more room than you think he needs.

Some casting exercises

When you first start casting you may tend to stiffen up because you are using muscles and movements which are strange to your

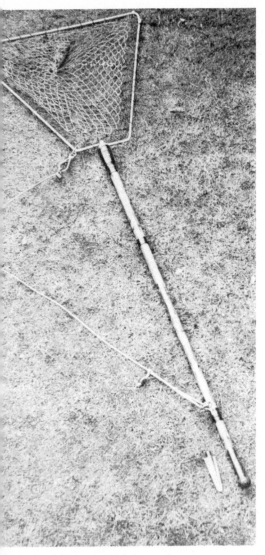

Photograph 32. For reservoir fishing a landing [net] needs to be simple in action and light to [car]ry. This one has a bamboo handle about 3′ 0″ [lon]g and the end stopper may be changed for the [me]tal spade. The net frame has a gape of 18″ [an]d the net is 24″ deep. The landing net is worn [usin]g by a stout cord, and a dog leash clip pro-vides a simple and quick release.

Photograph 33. I believe in travelling light. My tackle and oddments are carried in the waist bag or jacket pockets. This rod is a 15-year-old Hardy C.C. de France, very light and matched by a W F 6 F floating line on a Viscount reel.

Photographs 34 and 35. The contents of my waistbag (*above*) and of my waist-bag and jacket pockets (*below*). The bag is made on the lines of a large purse with a leather belt slotted through. From top left to bottom right in the photograph below: polaroid glasses, torch, cigar box holding lures and wet flies, plastic box holding dry flies, cigarette tin holding nymph patterns, beer mat leader carriers, detergent pad, floatant, Mucilin, Intrepid reel with S T 6 S Wet Cel shooting head, permit, safety pin, spare leaders in circular plastic carriers, plastic bags, cloth, priest, artery forceps, magnifier and trout spoon. The scissors are secured to my belt by a lanyard.

normal physical routine. The most likely parts to become tired will be the fingers, wrist and forearm on your casting side and most probably your shoulder muscles as well. Here are a few simple exercises which are well worth practising before the fishing season starts so that the muscles are prepared for longish spells of exercise under reservoir casting conditions.

1. Hold a tennis ball in the fingers of your rod hand and pinch it in and out about a dozen times. This will liven up the finger, wrist and forearm muscles.

2. Get the rake out of the garden shed and lay it flat on the ground in front of you. Pick up the handle with your rod hand. Keep your rod arm straight from shoulder to wrist and raise the rake gradually up from the ground to a horizontal position. Hold it there and then lower it gradually. You may not find this easy. Whatever you do don't overstrain but try to improve a little each day.

3. Get an empty long necked wine bottle and swing it from the shoulder holding the neck of the bottle clenched in your rod hand. Later on half fill the bottle with sand and repeat the dose until you can swing a whole bottle-full from the nine to three o'clock positions, keeping your wrist, forearm and elbow locked so that it is a whole arm movement from your shoulder joint.

These exercises may make you creak a bit to start with but will prove to be of good value when you have long spells of casting during a day's reservoir fishing.

Line control and retrieving

Once you have mastered your casting it is time to consider the next move which will lead to catching your trout. After a forward cast with a floating line you must first 'mend' the line so that it is dead straight. Keep you rod tip low to avoid wind resistance but always at an angle to the extended line. The reason for this is that if a fish makes a sudden 'take' at your fly your rod tip will flex and give to the initial pull. If your leader, line and rod are all in one line a sharp pull from a small fish will usually be enough to break the leader point.

If you want your fly to sink deeply, cast out, mend the line and count slowly up to about twenty. This will give the leader time to sink to its maximum, assuming it to be about nine or ten feet long. If fish are showing close to the surface then you must make a delicate cast—mend the line and simply allow the fly a few seconds to get into the top water layer.

Suggestions for fishing the different types of flies shown on the coloured frontispiece are described in the next chapter and the whole process of bringing the fly back at varying depths and speeds, whether it be a lure, wet fly or nymph, is called 'retrieving'. As the line is gathered back from the forward cast the forefinger of the rod hand is crooked round line and rod handle as in photograph 37 facing page 113 so that in the event of a 'take' you are able to tighten into your fish immediately. During windy weather you will find that your floating line develops a 'belly' on the water surface and this must be mended frequently so that you have a straight line between rod tip and leader, but always with the rod inclined at an angle to the line.

There are several ways of holding the line as it is retrieved with the line hand, but to start with it is easiest to let the retrieved line fall in broad coils onto the water or bankside. As an alternative, coil the retrieved line in loops of about 12" diameter and hold them loosely in your line hand. There is another very neat method of holding retrieved line known as 'figure of eight bunching'. This system is illustrated in figures 19A to 19E, reproduced from *Fly Fishing* by Maurice Wiggin, one of the 'Teach Yourself Books' published by the English Universities Press Ltd in 1958. I recommend our beginner to obtain a copy of this book. It is written in a very light-hearted style and the illustrations are excellent. Whichever system you adopt for holding the retrieved line, remember to keep your rod forefinger hooked over the line against the rod handle so that you may tighten immediately a fish makes an 'offer' or takes your fly.

Once you have mended the fly line following completion of the forward cast and allowed sufficient time for the fly to settle into the appropriate depth you must concentrate fully by watching the point at which the floating line tip meets the water. If there is any draw, deflection, dip, slowing down, jerk or other unusual movement, tighten immediately. It is at this point, where the floating line tip meets the water, that you are given a positive indication that something is interfering with the leader during retrieve. It could be that the fly hook has caught into a wisp of weed, but it could be a fish. In any case if you suspect a movement tighten immediately and you will know in less than a second whether it was weed or fish. If you

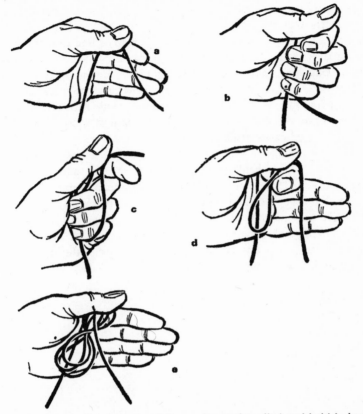

Figure 19. As the line is retrieved it may be neatly coiled and held in hand by this neat method called 'figure of eight bunching'. Drawings reproduced from *Teach Yourself Fly Fishing* by kind permission of Maurice Wiggin and of the publishers, English Universities Press Ltd.

have done any coarse fishing you will remember watching the float for signs of a take. In fly fishing the tip of your floating line may be regarded as the float—and if it quivers, tighten immediately.

If you see a fish rise close to your leader but feel nothing, tighten immediately. It is possible that he may have your fly in his mouth. Large trout can mouth a fly so delicately that there is little, if any, give-away signal at the floating line tip. On the other hand smaller fish are more inclined to snatch once they have decided to take the fly.

When fishing the sunk line the casting sequences we have analysed are exactly the same, but before you make a back cast you must be very sure to recover all but the last yard or so of line to relieve your rod of overstrain. Retrieving a thirty-yard sunk line can be by coiling or bunching, but where shooting heads are in use, the nylon cannot be coiled or bunched and most fishermen prefer to use some form of line raft to hold the retrieved nylon. Line rafts can be made to float upon the water or may be in the form of a pouch or basket secured to the caster's waist. The use of shooting heads is a skilled business, resulting in long distance casting, but as previously mentioned the 'double haul' casting sequence must be adopted for the best results and this is not included in the beginner's course.

The final aspects of line control and retrieve reach their peak when you have hooked your fish and he has to be played out and brought to the landing net. I shall leave over these aspects until later on when we examine a variety of situations which occur during bankside fishing at different times in a season.

6

Flies and Ways of Fishing Them

The word 'fly' is basically misleading. When people other than fisher-men talk about flies they are referring to the common house fly who has to be swatted out of the kitchen or perhaps the wretched blue-bottle trapped inside the car or even the midges which drive them mad towards the end of a pleasant evening's gardening during the summer months.

Fishermen's flies have been invented and developed by generations of fly tyers so as to imitate the widest possible variety of living creatures known to be of interest to the trout or other fish who may be deceived into taking a man-made artificial instead of nature's real thing.

Fly tying is an art of ever increasing popularity, and with the growth of reservoir fishing special patterns have been devised to interest and deceive the trout in these waters. Some beautifully illus-trated books have been published on this subject and I refer briefly to some of them in Appendix B, so that further information on natural fly life and the tying of matching artificials may be followed by those who wish to add to their enjoyment of reservoir fishing by learning to tie their own patterns.

The raw materials of the fly tyers include such diverse items as plumage from all kinds of birds, fur and hair from numerous animals stoats' tails, hares' ears, tinsel, wools of different dyes, floss, squirrels' tails, silks, nylon, beads, pieces of cork, fine copper wire, bits of poly-thene tube, varnish, wax etc. Add to these items the scales of hooks in differing lengths and sizes, couple these with the numerous hook shapes, and the permutations for making up artificials appear to be endless. One cursory look into the fly drawers of a large tackle display

85

must reveal at least a thousand different patterns and so where do we begin to select those which are going to be suitable for the reservoir bank fisherman?

In the first place let's re-cap and add to what I previously wrote about the reservoir trout's larder and his feeding habits. If our reservoir has been formed by flooding rich arable land there will be a great deal of bottom feed. Items in this class will include blood worms, fresh water snails, big garden worms and numerous other delicacies which, for the want of a better term, I refer to broadly as grubs. This type of food will support the trout adequately and in such reservoirs trout put on weight rapidly. As the sunshine re-appears after the long winter months the aquatic and land-bred insects will supplement the trout's larder. The marginal shallows will be generally productive, particularly where weeds can provide cover for the little creatures who have to struggle from their early homes in the silt or mud, making their way towards the water surface by climbing the stems of reeds until they rest suspended just below the surface film waiting for their emergence as an adult. During this process the trout will find an abundance of insect food. He will lie quietly just inside or on the outskirts of the marginal weed beds taking the nymphs and pupae as they struggle towards the water surface. He will either 'sip' the newly hatched surface fly or take it with a resounding whorl, particularly so if it happens to be a large one. It is worth mentioning that a newly hatched water fly may achieve 'lift-off' quite rapidly in some cases, particularly if the weather is dry and warm, but during drizzle it will take longer because he must wait for his wings to develop and dry out before he is able to fly. This fact has not escaped the notice of the trout, who will normally make a more leisurely rise during a drizzly day, as opposed to a much crisper one during bright sunshine. After the mature flies hatch from the surface, particularly around sunset on a warm evening, the mating carnival gets going and such is the joy of these mating flies that many pairs fall knotted to the water surface only to be sipped down by our old friend who knows this routine by heart. For the most part, the female insect leaves her mate and returns to lay her eggs upon the water surface. After this mission is complete she too falls victim to the cruising trout as she flutters weakly on the surface film. Many of the males take cover on land, but if wind is blowing towards the water they too will end their days as part of a trout's supper.

Quite apart from the luxuries of bottom feed and the gaiety of feeding upon the various forms of aquatic and land-bred insect life, the reservoir trout has another source of food which probably forms the greater part of his staple diet. This includes the stickleback and minnow brigades, and more important still the small coarse fish which sooner or later seem to find their way into most reservoirs no matter how carefully the inlet meshes and feeder streams are screened. The eggs of many coarse fish are carried on the webbed feet of various water birds and this is only one of the several ways by which small pike, perch, roach, rudd and gudgeon may set up home in a reservoir. The trout will forage wildly for small fish, and once he gets the taste for this type of feed he does not readily change his habits while it remains available. To supplement his larder the trout has yet another source of food—this includes water snail, fresh water shrimp, water boatmen, water louse and water fleas by the thousand, and as if not handsomely provided for without further addition the trout will quite often be presented by large numbers of land-bred insects blown on to the water and amongst these he will enjoy hawthorn flies, black gnats, winged ants, bracken beetles, daddy-long-legs and grass-hoppers.

With these very numerous types of creatures available to the reservoir trout, the fly tyer is faced with the task of making artificial patterns which will deceive the fish under varying conditions throughout the season. He succeeds by producing artificials, all classed as 'flies', which may be described as falling within the categories which follow; many of them have no relationship at all to nature's flies which actually fly in the air. His materials are carefully dressed, sometimes weighted (to assist sinking) whipped and finished to hooks of various shapes and sizes. Trout hooks are generally referred to in terms of size as recorded by the Redditch scale. This scale embraces numbers running from 6 to 18—No. 6 is a large size and No. 18 very small. A fly tyer's catalogue will aways quote the hook size and also the pattern.

The flies included in the coloured frontispiece as are follows:

Lures

Lures are generally tied on large hooks and are intended to rouse the trout's instinct to follow and eventually seize what he considers to be a small fish or other sizeable creature trying to escape. When small fish dash about and turn they cause a 'flash' as the light is reflected from their shiny flanks. For this reason most lures contain some silver or other bright or fluorescent material in their tying. Lures are generally fished deep, following a long cast with a sunk line or sinking shooting head. The method of retrieve is a most important part of the art of reservoir fishing. Remember that the reservoir fisherman seldom has any worthwhile current to move his fly and he must vary his style of retrieve from fast to very slow at various depths so as to impart a life-like movement into his artificial.

When lure fishing it usually pays to cast out a longish line and allow the fly to sink completely, and this may involve a pause of a minute or more. It can be retrieved either very fast by a continuous stripping movement by the line hand, or by a series of jerks and pauses. The first method will cause the lure to appear as a fast swimming small fish dashing for cover, and the second method would probably give the impression of an injured fish struggling about the place, both of which are usually good enough to interest a deep water trout.

A trout seems to have endless patience for following a lure and when he decides to take it there is usually a very positive snatch, though this snatch may be preceded by a series of plucks which are a sort of preliminary enquiry on behalf of the trout when investigating his prey. If these plucks continue it pays to be patient, because if a fish is really going to seize the lure the 'take' is generally a very positive affair and all the fisherman need do is to tighten immediately and get on terms with the fish. The Jersey Herd and Black and Peacock Tandem in the frontispiece are very reliable lures under most conditions. The former is generally fished fast and most probably deceives the trout into taking it as a small fish; the latter is best fished very slowly, with little jerks to impart the impression of life in a number of creatures whose silhouette is resembled in this tying. Both these lures were developed by T. C. Ivens, author of *Still Water Fly Fishing*. My inclusion of the Worm Fly under the heading of 'lures' may cause controversy. I do not know who invented it, neither do I know what it is intended to represent. Some say that when fished deep and slowly it has the outline of a large worm—and others that it was intended to represent a pair of knotted sedge flies who have found their way into the water after the mating carnival. Another fisherman at Blagdon told me that it was never tied to represent anything, but the trout find it of great interest and that is all that matters, and this is prob-

ably as good an explanation of its origin as any. I have caught fish
with this lure in very deep water moving it an inch or two at a time.
At Darwell and Bough Beech, when the big sedge flies come up, I
have fished it dry (well doused in silicone) and taken good fish by
this method. I have also taken fish by retrieving fast so as to make
the ridiculous thing 'skate' across the surface during the last half
hour of an evening's fishing. For me it is the complete standby and
an essential for Blagdon at any time. The pattern I use is as sold at
Woodford Lodge, Chew but a single hook tying is as good. This
lure will often save the day during a flat calm in mid-summer.
The method at that time is to cast out a fair distance using a floating
line and long leader. Let the lure sink fully and give the line an
occasional twitch. If you see the slightest response by way of movement at the point at which the floating line meets the water, tighten
immediately. It usually works.

Wet flies—attractors and deceivers

Under this broad heading are included some well-tried old faithfuls,
which although not tied to imitate any of nature's 'flying flies' have
proved their worth time and time again throughout the reservoir
fishing scene. No matter how well flies be tied it is of first importance
to present them to the fish at the correct *depth*. This may be a matter
of trial and error, but if fish are to be seen moving in the upper two
feet or so it is well worth a try to deceive them at this depth rather
than to fish the bottom in the hope that they are there too. If there
is nothing showing by way of fish movement then start deep and
gradually alter your style so that all layers of water are explored.
It is also essential to give serious thought to the question of fly *size*.
I am convinced that most of the flies we collect are too big for the
job. Please do not fall into the misunderstanding that big fish are only
caught on big flies. If you open up a trout and examine his stomach
contents you may find him stuffed with minnow, but on the other
hand he may be choked solid with minute midge pupae. Biggish flies
are fairly safe under rough water and dull light, but during bright
light it pays time and time again to fish very small flies on a long and
finely pointed leader.

The flies on the frontispiece under this heading include: Black
and Peacock Spider, Mallard and Claret, Dunkeld, Peter Ross, Silver
Invicta and Zulu. I give pride of place to the Black and Peacock

Spider as this is my favourite wet fly. As always, the depth and method of presentation are of first importance in fishing at any particular time. This fly is usually buoyant and fishes beautifully in the upper water levels. It must always be fished very slowly and is the complete deceiver for trout when they are stuffing themselves with water snail and other grubs. This fly is best fished with floating line tactics and it can be deadly when fished about 18" under the surface towards or after the end of a good evening rise. The Mallard and Claret, Dunkeld, Peter Ross, Silver Invicta and Zulu all have an element of 'flash' about them and can be fished fast to imitate small fry, but as always, at the appropriate depth depending upon conditions. The Mallard and Claret is a great taker at Blagdon and Chew, and the Silver Invicta and Zulu are very good deceivers to use when trout are swimming fast and high in a forage for stickleback or coarse fish fry. These wet flies may be worked by either sunk line or floating line. My preference is for a floating line with a long leader so that depth may be varied by adjustment in leader presentation. It is essential to adapt your fishing methods to prevailing conditions and, in short, to fish where the fish are likely to be and at the correct depth.

Buzzer patterns

In this category I have selected patterns in the frontispiece which have proved to be most satisfactory in my experience. When fishing these, we are trying to deceive the trout into taking the feeble and slowly struggling underwater creature who is making his way up from the silt or weed bed towards the surface prior to setting himself up in readiness for 'lift-off'.

If you look into the shallows you can often see these little fellows struggling around—they try to lash about in a sort of wriggling upward movement and every now and again they seem to run out energy and drop down a few inches. Then they have another go and by a series of such attempts they eventually reach some reed stem or other landing stage just below the water surface, where they hang beneath the surface film waiting for final emergence as the winged adult. These little creatures are of tremendous importance to the trout, who will lie or patrol quietly, high in the water, taking in the struggling pupae for a pastime. There is one particular family of such insects which is of very great importance to the trout and in consequence to the fisherman also. This family rejoice in the name of Chironomidae and according to John Goddard in his masterly book *Trout Flies of Still Water* (A. & C. Black) there are over 380 British species in this family, mainly of aquatic origin. The fishermen have nicknamed these insects 'buzzers'. The larger flies of this family adopt a hooked shape, particularly the females as they drift about the water surface on their egg-laying mission. The eggs are laid in a sort of jelly and they gradually reach the bottom of the water, where the life cycle begins. The buzzers vary in colour from black to green to red and during their early life the larvae, known as blood worms, live in little mud tubes on the silty patches of the reservoir bottom. These blood worms are much savoured by the trout, who will frequently stir up the mud in order to sort them out. In their next stage the buzzer pupae develop little breathing tubes and they stand upright swaying about on the bottom rather like happy drunkards, particularly in undisturbed marginal waters. Before the adult fly (midge) can emerge the pupae must ascend to the surface—again a fact which has not escaped the notice of the trout who, far from being interested in preserving the future of a species, takes these suspended pupae with great delight and very considerable delicacy. The emergence of the adult midge is usually a rapid affair and off they fly to take cover on land, prior to mating and a final return of the females for egg-laying. Although the adult midges hatch fairly rapidly they are not always quick enough to avoid being sucked down by the trout lying just under the surface in readiness for this occasion. In order to deceive the trout feeding on buzzers in their various stages some very useful patterns have been devised and these are included on the frontispiece. The Red Larva imitates the blood worm stage, the Footballer is a very successful pattern for imitating the pupa and this fly was developed by Geoffrey Bucknall, author of *Fly Fishing Tactics on Still Water* (Muller), another book for the beginner to put on his list for further study and to which I refer in Appendix B. The larger Black Buzzer is a fairly standard pattern used with success on many reservoirs and for me this tying has always served well under the right conditions. Buzzer tactics require a very delicate approach because in this type of fishing we are trying to deceive the trout into taking a feeble and slowly moving creature in different stages of its life cycle. For the Red Larva the sunk line may be used, or better still a floating line with a leader at least twelve feet long. The fly must be allowed to sink fully and it is 'worked' by giving the line a series of little jerks during a very long and slow retrieve about an inch at a time.

When trout are feeding on midge pupae they become very pre-occupied and the rise form usually results in a slow but deliberate head and tail movement with the tip of the dorsal fin just breaking the water surface. Fishing for these is really delicate work and calls for a floating line tip and long leader tapered to as fine a point as you dare risk with perhaps one or two dropper links. The leader should be greased to within 3" of the point but the droppers must be left ungreased. Tie a Black Buzzer on the point and a smaller Footballer on each dropper. Cast out, straighten the line and let the leader remain stationary in the area of surface feeding. The droppers will be 'hanging' just under the surface film and the heavier point fly will be about three to four inches beneath the surface. A 'take' will result in a slight movement at the point at which the floating line meets the leader and you must tighten immediately. Likewise if a fish rises anywhere near the leader tighten—because he may already have your fly in his mouth. This type of fishing can be very rewarding but it demands a considerable degree of concentration and you must be prepared to tighten at the slightest hint of a take, because the trout feeding on these creatures do so with great delicacy and very little surface disturbance.

Nymphs

The patterns included on the colour plate are the Ivens Brown, Ivens Green and Brown, and Ivens Green. I need hardly add that these are all patterns devised by the author of *Still Water Fly Fishing* —and they really are perfect deceivers when fished as the author advises. Where fish are seen to be feeding in the upper water layers either of these artificials is always worth a try. As always, depth and method of presentation are the essential factors and a floating line coupled with a leader of about ten feet with a single point fly is probably best for the Ivens Brown and Ivens Green patterns. The former is always worth a try when sedge flies are hatching because the tying probably deceives the trout into taking it as a sedge pupa. The green pattern has done well for me in the five to eight feet depth regions—always with floating line and a leader well soaked with detergent to encourage easy sinking. The Green and Brown patterns can be used with success when fish are swimming high in the water on stickleback-chasing missions. Use a leader with two dropper links and tie on a Green and Brown to each dropper and a third on the point also. Cast out your floating line to cover the general line being worked by the fish, and once he starts moving bring the flies back in the upper 12" of water at a fair pace. He may make a mistake and you will usually have a good fish if he does. I most strongly recommend a beginner to make a very careful study of the methods advocated by Mr Ivens for fishing the flies he has devised. These flies are not tied to imitate natural insect forms, but they will deceive the trout time and time again when fished in a suitable size, at the correct depth, and with variable methods of retrieve so as to impart life-like movement.

The last three nymph patterns included are all as devised by Frank Sawyer who has covered the entire field of nymph fishing in his book *Nymphs and the Trout* published by A. & C. Black in 1970. The patterns chosen are all as tied by Mrs Sawyer at Salisbury, Wiltshire, and each contains fine copper wire so that it sinks instantly upon reaching the water surface. Fishing a leaded nymph can be very rewarding in reservoirs using the floating line and a longish leader tapered to a fine point. Towards the end of 1967 I wrote to Mr Sawyer asking his advice upon certain aspects of this type of fishing and here is part of his reply which he kindly sent me and has given me permission to quote:

'I think you will find each of these patterns attractive if fished in the right way, but I usually pin my faith to what we call the Grayling Lure. Fishing with a single leaded nymph on a long leader with a fine point is my practice. Nymph fishing in still waters can be fascinating. All our patterns are constructed to sink readily. When fishing them, just cast to the area of a rising fish. Allow the nymph to sink and then very slowly work it in towards you. Watch closely from the moment the nymph strikes the water and sinks. Your attention must be on the floating line and leader which should ride high in the surface. Watch carefully the point where the leader enters the water. Should it check in its drift, drawn down, or jerk then tighten quickly. The take of a trout, even a big one, can be very delicate and often your only indication is the movement of the floating leader or line. You cannot be too quick.'

In an article in *Trout and Salmon* which preceded Mr Sawyer's advice to me, he made the great point that as part of the art of fishing a leaded nymph you must gently raise the tip of your rod to give animation to the nymph. After each gentle rod tip lift, retrieve the spare line, lower the rod tip and very gently but deliberately repeat the process. In this way the nymph will be made to rise and fall very slowly in the water and this movement could be of such interest to a watching trout that it may *induce* a take. You will see that Mr Sawyer advised that 'the leader should ride high on the surface'. To achieve this a little Mucilin applied for about three feet along the butt will help—and even further towards the leader point if fish are obviously feeding in the topmost layer of water.

Dry flies

In my opinion there is not nearly enough attention paid to the sport which may be obtained from dry fly fishing from the banks of reservoirs. In the next chapter is some more detailed advice for those who wish to pursue this fascinating aspect of reservoir fishing—but for the present we are dealing with the flies appearing on the colour plate.

The Black Gnat is a beautiful fly for fishing dry on a dull day. He sits up and can be seen by both fisherman and fish. He is best fished at the edge of a ripple amongst the naturals which will be blown to the same line where the wind meets the water. The Sedge pattern will serve as a fair imitation for a variety of the naturals and can be fished with great success on the edge of a reed bed where trout sometimes lie in no more than 18" of water taking the sedge flies, just before they fly off from the water surface. At dusk this pattern well doused with silicone can be made to 'skate' across the water by a continuous retrieve, and this movement will frequently enrage a trout who will not bother about line wake in order to seize the artificial. Alternatively the dry sedge may be cast out and left to wander on the ripple edge, with an occasional 'tweak' given to the floating line which imparts a little life-like movement in the fly.

The dry Coch-y-Bonddu imitates the beetle which is blown in masses from the banks of some reservoirs, particularly where bracken and gorse bushes grow near the waterside. His silhouette is sharp and clear under dull conditions, and just as the Black and Peacock Spider imitates the actions of many underwater creatures so does this pattern interest the surface feeding trout. The Hatching Midge is the winged adult of the buzzer family. Buzzers hatch at intervals throughout the day on most reservoirs though their main activity appears to be at dusk. This pattern will serve as a general imitator if you want to try your hand at deceiving the trout on the dry fly when it is obvious that there is some general buzzer activity on the water—enough to bring about this type of selective feeding which I described when dealing with the buzzer patterns. The dry flies are best fished with leaders at least twelve feet in length tapered to as fine a point as you dare risk. The floating line must be straightened or mended at intervals so that there is no pronounced curve in the line between rod tip and fly. The rod tip is best kept low to prevent wind resistance but *never* have the tip of the rod in direct alignment with the fly line. This advice applies equally to wet fly, nymph or dry fly fishing and the reason is this. If a fish makes a sudden snatch at your fly, with leader, line and rod all in one line a break is almost certain. A sudden take by a small fish will be enough—let alone one from a large fish. The trick is to keep your rod tip low but always at an angle to the fly line so that when a sudden take occurs the strain is taken by the flexing of the rod tip.

Good stand-bys

The last three sets of flies on the colour plate are conveniently described under this type of heading. The Shrimper and Sedge Pupa are as recommended by John Goddard. Trout do not eat many fresh water shrimps in the summer time but they devour great quantities during the winter. However, they are quite capable of being deceived into taking the Shrimper, particularly in shallow bays where there are weed beds and stones. On some reservoirs, although there may be an abundance of sedge flies, the trout will often refuse the dry sedge but can more frequently be taken by the Sedge Pupa fished just under the surface. If you are fishing a dry sedge pattern and rise a trout who refuses the fly then try him with a Sedge Pupa or an Ivens Brown—he may well take either. The Corixa patterns are as tied by Les Sawyer, the bailiff at Bough Beech. These are deceivers for use when the trout is after the water boatmen who appear in the shallows of most reservoirs. All the flies under this heading are best fished with floating line, a longish leader, fine point and single fly. The Sedge Pupa is best fished in the upper layer of water but the Shrimper and Corixa patterns must be allowed to sink gradually and then be fished with the type of rod top movement described in connection with leaded nymph tactics. Remember—we are again trying to give the artificials a little life-like wobble and variations in depth, to imitate the naturals. The Corixa are little beetle-like creatures with keel-shaped backs with a shiny surface. Some are brown, others more yellow and others greenish. A fluorescent tying has proved to be successful and small sizes are essential if the deception is to be complete. Some little jerky movement is best imparted into the fishing method to imitate the way in which the naturals rise and fall in the shallow waters.

To summarize, the main points to be borne in mind on the selection and presentation of flies when fishing from a reservoir bank are broadly as follows:

1. There is no need to worry a great deal about selecting a fly on the basis of exact imitation of the insect or other creature on which you have judged the trout to be feeding at any given time.

2. It is quite all right to tie on a pattern which you think is a fair representation but it is absolutely essential to fish the fly of your choice a at the correct depth, b with a retrieve varying from very fast to a mere wobble depending upon the pace and style of movement adopted by the natural creature you have in mind at the time and c with a hook size judged suitable to complete the deception.

3. When fishing dry flies, nymphs and pupae patterns avoid wading whenever possible to minimize disturbance of valuable marginal water. Take advantage of any background cover and spend time watching before starting to fish. You will get tremendous enjoyment out of these styles of fishing provided you are prepared to give them full concentration. Use as long a leader as you can manage with as fine a point as you feel able to risk having regard to the probable weight of fish in your reservoir. Under calm water conditions get down on one knee well back from the water's edge to avoid disturbance by vibration or shadow.

4. Practice rod top lift coupled with careful line retrieve to present your artificial at varying depths. The resultant movement in your fly may very well prove to be the deciding factor in whether or not a trout will take. He must be tempted to take interest.

5. If you are convinced that you have found a quiet spot where you would expect trout to feed then give it a very thorough working-

over in a methodical manner. Reckon to spend about two hours fishing a spot where you are confident of finding fish, and be prepared to try every method from dry fly, nymph, wet fly and lure at their respective depths before deciding that you are wrong and it is time to look elsewhere.

6. If your casting is out of form do not upset a good fishing spot by thrashing the water, which must result in scaring away the trout. Have a rest, sit down and sort out where you are making mistakes, make a few practice casts along the bank, and once you have worked out the fault resume your fishing with renewed confidence.

Finally, never forget that you have taken up this sport for pleasure. If you have had a day's outing without catching a fish don't let it get you down. Remember the good casts you made under difficult conditions and think about those three fish you rose but which were not quite right in timing for hooking—the fact that you deceived them into rising to your fly shows you are more than half way there. Next time they'll be in the bag.

Fly sizes

There are no hard and fast rules governing the precise size to which an artificial must be tied. Lures are generally tied large on hooks of sizes 6 to 8 and wet flies are usually in the size 8 to 14 bracket. Sizes 10 to 14 are the most useful for general nymph patterns but when a very small midge pupa or pheasant tail nymph is considered necessary then size 16 will be required. Dry fly patterns tied between sizes 10 to 14 are generally suitable for reservoir work but occasionally size 16 dry flies may be needed, and as a complete contrast two very large dark bushy dry flies will be useful for the·tactics described in chapter 8. During bright light it pays to use small flies and nymph patterns tied to fine points on a long leader, but during conditions of dull light or heavy ripple larger sizes may prove more effective.

(*Note* : Of the flies included on the frontispiece the Ivens-type patterns, the dry flies and those devised by John Goddard were obtained from Messrs Benwoods of London N.W.8 and the wet fly patterns are as supplied by Messrs C. Farlow and Co. Ltd, London S.W.1.)

7

Fishermen and Fishing Methods

This chapter deals with the value of meeting other fishermen and outlines the opportunities for practising different styles of fishing during the course of a season.

As you become more interested in your new sport of reservoir fishing you are bound to make friends with fishermen of far greater experience. A beginner starts with no knowledge at all, and as a result of varied reading and muddling along experience is gradually acquired. This acquisition of experience can be a long and frustrating business and the best way of short circuiting the whole process is to find a friend who is already an experienced fly fisherman. I was particularly fortunate in this respect because out of a chance meeting in the fishing hut at Durleigh in Somerset during a heavy thunderstorm one afternoon in May 1963, I had the greatest good fortune to meet Mr John Burgess and his charming wife Margot, both of whom are very experienced in all types of angling and particularly so in bank fishing for reservoir trout. I believe John is the oldest season ticket holder at Durleigh. He has at least fifty years of fishing experience behind him and throughout his life has fished the rivers, streams, lakes and reservoirs of Devon and Somerset. He is now happily retired and fishes mainly at Clatworthy, a beautiful reservoir high up in the Brendon Hills above Minehead, and also at Blagdon, that beautiful lake which maintains such fine trout year after year. From our chance meeting in 1963 we became great friends and I have no hesitation in saying that I have learnt more about reservoir trout fishing from John and Margot than from any other source. Unfortunately the distance between our respective homes limits our fishing days to no more than a few each season, but these are the days to which I most look forward. In my experience the best fly fishermen are usually rather quiet and modest but once you can get them to open up on the subject, making it clear you are a beginner and anxious to obtain a little more information to help you on your way, there is no limit to the time they are prepared to give towards helping. So when you start fishing regularly at your reservoir allow yourself plenty of time to watch the way more experienced anglers go about their work. If you get the chance of a day out with a really good fisherman, grab it and go. A few hours' instruction at the waterside with an experienced fisherman guiding your next move will teach you more than a winter time of reading, but this is not to say that the reading is wasted. It forms an essential part of every angler's background knowledge.

I have explained there are really two schools of bank fishermen. There are those who prefer to select a spot where trout are known to cruise and feed, and to cover a very wide arc of water by skilled long distance casting methods—adopting a floating or sinking shooting head coupled with the double haul system of casting. Make no mistake about it, many of these fishermen take tremendous bags of fish during the course of a season and their tactics demand a high degree of endurance and long casting skill. On the other hand you have the 'roaming' type of bank fisherman who prefers to explore the more distant and less fished parts of the water, carrying the minimum of tackle for mobility and trying out odd spots which appeal to him as being likely holding grounds for trout. During a day's fishing this chap will cover several miles of shore line and his fishing methods will be adapted to suit the depth of water at each selected stretch of the reservoir bank. A few reservoir fishermen have achieved top class recognition by becoming complete all-rounders. They are few and far between and much to be envied. The top class all-rounder in this sport is able to cast a large fly or lure forty yards or more when required, then change style completely and take a cruising fish on a dry midge cast from a kneeling position ten yards over a weed bed, and the next day get afloat and catch his limit by the varied styles of boat fishing. It takes many years to reach these standards, but the great thing about this game is that there are endless approaches to catching a trout under reservoir conditions and they must vary tremendously from one part of the country to another.

Some reservoirs are open for fishing in April, and we will now look at the various styles of fishing which may be used from then on.

Fishing deep

At the beginning of a season starting in April the fish will be recovering from a hard winter and with very few exceptions the trout will tend to be at the bottom in deep water. There are two approaches for getting a fly down to the appropriate depth. You can use either a forward taper or double taper sinking line of standard thirty yard length, or a fast sinking shooting head of about thirty feet in length backed by nylon or braided terylene. If you decide to use a shooting head it is not necessary to be able to cast by the double haul system if you are content with a twenty-five yard cast, so you can use the same casting methods as we analysed previously. The fish will generally tend to be sluggish and must have their interests roused, perhaps by use of the following flies and methods—using a leader of not less than twelve feet in length which with the sinking line or shooting head must be allowed to submerge completely before beginning a retrieve. This may involve a wait of a minute or more depending upon shore line conditions and water depth.

1. Worm fly or Jersey Herd fished deep with short jerky retrieves.

2. Jersey Herd fished deep and stripped in very fast with occasional pauses so that this heavy fly has time to sink towards the bottom in between spells of fast retrieve.

3. Black and Peacock Tandem fished deep and moved very, very slowly—just about three inches of retrieve then a pause. Vary this with a retrieve of about one yard then allow the lure to sink down again. This form of retrieve is known as the 'sink and draw' method.

4. Add a dropper to the leader about one yard back from the point. Tie on a Dunkeld dropper and Peter Ross at the point. Let the line sink fully and retrieve in short sharp jerks; remember that with flies of this type and the Jersey Herd you are trying to simulate the flash and movement of small fish.

There are many lure patterns which have been designed to arouse the trout's interest in small fish—the Polystickle, Muddler Minnow and Sinfoil Fry to name but three. Have a word with the bailiff of your reservoir and see which types he advises. After all he is the man who sees all the fishing returns and knows which lures have taken most fish and quite apart from this aspect he has probably tied several of his own patterns which, through his general fishing knowledge, will usually do the trick. At this time of the year the fish have got to be made to move and respond to a fly. Depth and method of presentation are the prime factors, coupled with knowing where the fish are likely to be at the outset of the season. Some detailed study of the reservoir map will be a help because it is almost sure to show the contrasting areas of deep and shallow water and for this early season fishing the deeper water will give a better chance for success. Try the corners of dams, and if you have a deep short line of scoured out rock or gravel, fish these areas very thoroughly with the Black and Peacock Spider; remember how deadly this fly is for the water snail imitation and how many other creatures it resembles in silhouette, enough at any rate to interest the trout. Fish it deep and very slowly.

When a trout becomes interested in a deeply fished lure he will follow it for a long time. He may make one or two plucks at it and then a decisive snatch. The trout usually hooks himself on the snatch and all that remains is for the fisherman to take control. A rainbow trout will usually rush madly away and probably make several spectacular leaps from the surface despite the heavy line behind him. If he wants to run and he is a powerful fish, let him, but do not let him fight and thrash about on the surface; give him line so that he works off his energy in deeper water. As soon as possible get the line back on to the reel so that he can take his next run against the reel check. If you are fishing from the bank as opposed to wading this action can be achieved rapidly by moving backwards up the bank to get a tight line in the minimum amount of time. Put on the pressure gradually, keep the rod vertical and you will feel its tremendous power as the tip flexes with each movement of the fish. Give the fish plenty of time and keep still. When you have him tiring and about ten yards away get your net extended forward with the whole of the net frame at least twelve inches under the water surface. If the fish wants to run again let him but keep a tight line. This time he seems to be running out of steam so reel in gradually keeping the rod perfectly upright and draw the fish towards you by a slow but deliberate backward movement of the rod. The fish has turned over on his side and this is usually a sign that he has had enough.

Unclip the landing net and rest the frame on the water bed with the handle pointing up to your middle. This leaves both hands free for reeling and playing the fish, and when he is ready for netting take the net handle from your middle and raise the net gape so that it is lying level but about twelve inches under the water surface—ready for the fish to glide in. Any clumsy work with a net, trying to shovel the fish in, can be disastrous. Each movement needs to be careful but positive and you must keep still. The lure which he took in this case is right in the corner or 'scissors' of his jaw. He is obviously well above the size limit for the regulations so take out the priest, hold the fish firmly across his back and strike his skull three times very accurately and sharply. It's all over and you have a fine rainbow on the bank. To your amazement you find that the lure has dropped out of the corner of his jaw and is caught in the mesh of the landing net. One hook of the tandem has been bent to just under dead straight and this is the hook which held him. If he had made one more run the chances are that the hook hold would have given and you would have lost a 3 lb rainbow. There is always a time when a decision has to be made whether you are going to put the strain on or is the fish to be allowed another run? In this case we seem to have made the right decision, but only just.

Not so deep

As an alternative to sunk line fishing in early spring the floating line can be used successfully on occasions. If you have knowledge of fish lying in say eight feet of water, use a twelve foot leader thoroughly doused in detergent and tie on one, two or even three of your favourite wet fly patterns. Clip on a split lead shot about 3" above the point fly. Cast out and allow plenty of time for the leader to sink to its maximum depth. The lead shot will assist sinking—but you must count slowly up to at least twenty-five before beginning a retrieve. Vary the retrieve from little jerks to sink and draw. You have three flies fishing at three different depths. If a fish takes the top dropper you will know that they are not so low down as you thought, so continue fishing at the lesser depth. The whole problem centres around depth and method of retrieve, plus the use of an attractor or deceiver pattern of fly.

Here is another suggestion for April fishing when there are no signs of surface movement at all. Find a spot where rough water is hitting a high bank or dam face causing foam slicks and cloudy water. Use a floating line and nine-foot leader. Tie on a Black and Peacock Spider at the point. Cast out about fifteen yards and let the leader sink. Do not retrieve, just let the line wander on the surface. The rough water will ripple the floating line which in turn will work the fly up and down to and from the embankment just under the frothy water. This method gave me six fish in under an hour on one occasion. They were all filled with water snail and once again a Black and Peacock Spider proved to be the complete deceiver. There was a hailstorm running during most of this activity as well. As an alternative use the floating line with a twelve-foot leader and tie on a Jersey Herd which the fly tier has weighted to assist quick sinking. Cast out, straighten the line and count slowly for twenty seconds so that the lure sinks before beginning a sharp and jerky retrieve. You must watch the crucial point where the tip of the floating line meets the leader because it is there that you will have your first sign of a fish taking interest. As you watch the line tip about eighteen yards out during a careful retrieve you think it has slowed slightly. Tighten! and immediately you feel the tug of a strong fish as he tears up towards the surface. You see him make two leaps and suddenly the line goes completely loose. Three seconds later a fish leaps out of the water only three yards away from your left wader. Your line is pathetically slack and you feel completely confused. What has happened? You felt a strong pull, this was followed by two leaps which you saw and felt about eighteen yards out, then the line went slack. And what about the fish you saw about three yards to your left? Probably what happened was this. First your lure was taken savagely and you saw your hooked fish leap twice at about the eighteen-yard mark. Your line then went slack because the fish was rushing *towards* you. Once he felt free of the tight line he made that leap three yards to your left, only a yard or so from the bank, and there was sufficient slack line for his leap to free the hook hold. What should you have done? The answer here lies in getting a tight line in the quickest possible manner. Once you felt the line go slack you should have stripped in the slack line with the fastest speed possible. Really haul it down the rod yards at a time and let it fall where it will and at the same time hold the rod high above your shoulder to reduce the length of slack to a minimum. By taking this instantaneous action it is possible you could have made contact with the fish before he had time to make that leap when the line was slack. When a fish is lost you are bound to feel fed up and there is a temporary loss of confidence. But look at it another way. In the first place you did very well to spot the very slight give-away movement at the line tip, and you also did well to tighten so smartly and were dead right in assessing that it was a fish which had interrupted the retrieve. The fact that you lost your fish because you did not know what to do when he rushed inshore could hardly be helped, because you had never experienced this problem before. There are very many ways of losing fish and this one is fairly common, so make a note of it for the future. I should add that reel manufacturers have done a great deal towards overcoming this cause of lost fish as there are some modern reels which, by the flick of a lever, will take in yards of slack in a second. These reels are excellent for experienced fishermen but are not suitable for a beginner.

It's warming up: wet fly and nymph

As the season moves on into May, the water will be warming up gradually and in consequence the aquatic insect life will start interesting the trout. Occasional rises will be seen, particularly towards midday and early afternoon when at this time of the year it is warmer than early morning or evening. If you have been catching fish with your sunk line tactics during the preceding weeks you may decide to continue with this method—because if fish are showing at the surface occasionally there is more than an even chance they will be moving in deeper water as well; but for my money I shall put away the sunk line for a while and concentrate on floating line tactics. Let's have a look at some of the possibilities.

First it will pay to travel light and walk well away from the areas which have been heavily fished so far, and this may mean a pleasant walk of a mile or two up the reservoir bank. Keep well away from any car parking areas because the water there is always well and truly flogged by fishermen who quite naturally want to get going with the minimum delay upon arrival and by others returning from more distant parts who think 'I'll just have a dozen casts more by the car park before packing up'. The conditions are good for today's fishing—let's say you are on the west bank and there is a mild south-westerly wind, not at all strong but just enough to create a ripple about ten yards off the shore line. It is overcast but every now and then the sun peeps through and you can feel the warmth. Just a little drizzle occasionally, not hard driving rain but enough to agitate the water surface. You have passed several fishermen on your way and have reached a bay which, judging by the few footprints around the margins has not been fished much this season. This bay is fairly sheltered but there are a number of bushes around the perimeter which will make it necessary to keep a high back cast if you are to fish without wading. Sit down and see if there are any signs of fish moving. After a few minutes several swifts sweep across the bay, which is only about thirty yards wide at its mouth, and the birds dip to take some fly or other off the water. This goes on fairly steadily. A fish makes a gentle rise about fifteen yards offshore and more or less to your front. Then another rise occurs about five yards upwind of the last but still on the same line, about fifteen yards offshore. It seems that the fish have found something to interest them in the upper water layer and there is a fairly regular pattern of 'humping' rises along this line. The sun has gone behind cloud and seems unlikely to come out for some while. It is generally overcast, but still mild. A dark fly will probably attract the fish under these conditions and it is fairly obvious that there are trout moving and feeding in the upper water levels about fifteen yards out. These are Black and Peacock Spider conditions and I suggest you try this fly, about size 12, with a twelve-foot leader tapered to a fine point, but the leader must be well soaked in detergent to assist instant sinking. The Black and Peacock Spider is a buoyant fly and will fish well in the upper water. Any wading will certainly put the fish down and it will be necessary to keep a high back cast to clear those bushes which are only a few yards behind. There are one or two useful gaps which give a chance for a fair back cast, so have a go. Strip out plenty of line and let it fall neatly near your feet, do not tread on it, and keep it free from bits of twig and weed. The first cast will give the best chance and any false casting must be done carefully to avoid slapping the water otherwise these trout will go down for a certainty. Off you go with some neat and tidy false casting, looking back over the rod shoulder to ensure that the line on the back cast is high and clear of the bushes and at the final shoot you are on target. Straighten the line. The leader sinks like a stone and you think how worthwhile it was giving it that good stretching when tying it on at the car park. It always pays to stretch a leader thoroughly by giving it some real tension and it will straighten out on delivery, particularly if tied with a long level butt of heavy nylon. In this type of wet fly fishing you are not casting to individual fish but are 'fishing the water', in other words making a methodical search in an area where fish are known to be feeding and moving. Start a very slow retrieve, with the fly about one foot under the surface, and watch the tip of your fly line as it bobbles about in the ripple during the retrieve. Nothing doing on the first retrieve, and when the line is about six yards from the rod tip go for a high back cast with a sharp left hand haul, make a good forward punch and out shoots the spare line in one go. Straighten the line and watch the tip. A slight draw downwards—tighten! Too late. That was a fish all right but you were too slow. Will there be another chance? Or have you had it as a result of that mess which occurred due to the line and leader coming back in a heap when the fish was missed? Keep calm and first check the hook barb. It is all right, so is the fly knot, and by some miracle the leader has not tangled. There is a lot to be said for tying that long thickish butt as it helps leaders to straighten out on delivery and avoids tangles. Coil up the spare line and move about ten yards away to some undisturbed spot on the same fifteen-yard line where, despite the previous trouble, the odd rise is still to be seen. Keep quiet and do not wade into the shallow water. A neat false casting sequence and out you go again. Straighten the line and watch the line tip like a heron. A very slow retrieve about two inches at a time, a slight dip at the point—tighten! and this one is on. He bores deep and there is no surface leaping or acrobatics but he is a strong fish and wants to run. You have a tight line and fish, leader, line, rod and you are all in one piece. Down and away he goes in a sort of outward semi-circular direction. Probably a useful brown trout. They do not often leap about like the rainbows but generally try to bore down deep. This one has the rod well flexed and you have the butt vertical and almost housed into your navel. He seems to be running out of energy and you gradually reel him in very firmly but positively, keeping the rod dead upright with the top flexing against the fish. Do not hurry. Keep a tight line and unclip the landing net, lay it on the bank which is about fifteen inches above the water here and make sure the net gape is free of the frame. Get down on one knee but keep that rod vertical. The fish is now five yards out and he has turned on his side. Lower the net into the water and keep the frame completely submerged. Lever the rod back over your shoulder and in a continuous backward movement of the rod guide the fish over the net. Raise the net and in he glides cleanly into the deep gape. This is a fine brown trout well over two pounds with brilliant orange and gold spots, a small head and deep body. Take out the priest and hold the fish firmly; give two or three sharp taps over his skull and it is all over. The Black and Peacock Spider is lodged firmly right in the trout's jaw. A quick nick with the scissors and it comes free without any damage to the hook or barb. Well done. You are really getting the idea of watching that floating line tip and tightening at the slightest hint of an offer from the fish. This demands concentration and a quick reflex. The high back casting was good also. That business with the ladder in the back garden was worthwhile after all. A sharp left hand haul enabled you to keep the back cast high, thus avoiding the bushes which were quite close behind. Your brown trout was taken in the upper water level on the Black and Peacock Spider. It is quite probable that an equally good result could have been achieved with an Ivens Brown or Ivens Green nymph because at this time of the year the fish are really feeding hard, and as long as you use a deceiver pattern of suitable size fished at the correct depth, and vary the line retrieve to give the fly animation, you will always stand a very good chance of success. This is not an easy bay to fish. Wading would have scared the fish out and a low back cast with consequent tangling in the bushes would have wasted valuable fishing time and upset your confidence. Rest again and see whether there are still signs of fish moving near the surface. It seems to have gone quiet and those periodic rises are no longer the pattern. It is getting really warm and the sun is peeping through the odd gaps in the cloud. You are still the only fisherman up in this bay. You know fish feed here and under these conditions stay put and watch a while. All of a sudden you see a tremendous whorl in the surface about ten yards out. That must have been a good fish and it seemed as though he took something off the surface with a really sudden swirl. His rise has caused circular ripples which travel away five yards or more from where you first saw him. There is another over to the left and still about ten yards out. As you look across the water you can see several sedge flies hovering and dipping just above the surface. It seems there is a hatch of insects and those two fish may have taken similar flies just as they were on the point of 'lift-off'. If this is the case a dry fly may lead to success, and this would be a good time to add a little about dry fly fishing when bank fishing for reservoir trout.

Dry fly

For every fish I catch on the dry fly I must miss at least ten but strangely enough this does not stop me dry fly fishing, because under the right conditions fish can be deceived time and time again, provided the fisherman has mastered this part of the reservoir fishing art. I rise but miss fish because I tighten too soon or too late, but as the seasons go on I hope to get it right. If my main concern were catching as many fish as possible it would be far better to stick to lure, wet fly and nymph tactics but dry fly fishing fascinates me and since I go fishing for enjoyment I always have a go at this method when it is obvious that the fish are taking surface feed. My friend John Burgess is a master of dry fly fishing and is consistently successful, as the record books of several West Country reservoirs will verify. I have talked to him for hours on this subject and watched him fish his style over a period of years. The main points to bear in mind are as follows.

Reservoirs formed by flooding rich arable land will generally contain a great assortment of bottom feed, but after a few years the aquatic insect cycle will become generally established and once fish can be seen rising to take hatching flies or land-bred insects blown from the bank out over the water the chance is there for the fisherman who wants to pursue dry fly fishing. In the first place mobility is essential; you must be prepared to wander to the less fished parts and it will pay to sit quietly and watch for signs of surface feeding. Keep a look-out for signs of insect life. It may be that hawthorn or other land-bred flies are being blown over the water, or perhaps you have spotted a hatch of sedge flies or midges coming up from the water surface. On a brightish day the chances of a trout rising are most likely just at the time when a cloud passes across the sun taking the brightness off the water; remember, he sees particularly well in dull light. Exact imitation of the type of fly in question is not essential, but your chances of success towards deceiving the trout will increase if you can present him with an artificial of about the same size as that in which you have judged him to be interested and more still if the silhouette of your fly as seen from the trout's window is as near to the natural insect as possible. The dry flies you use must be tied with good stiff hackles and must sit up on the water as naturally as possible. The flies must be well doused with silicone or other floatant so that they do not become drowned in a lively ripple. If the fly will not sit on the water properly it is useless and must be discarded. Ripple-edge fishing is usually the most productive for dry fly work, but above all it is essential that the light is such that the fisherman can see his fly from the time it makes its neat and delicate landing until taken by the fish or brought back for a fresh cast. A long leader of about twelve to fifteen feet is best and the point of the leader must be as fine as you dare risk having regard to the probable weight of the fish you are after. The leader must be either completely dry or lightly greased and it must straighten out completely at the forward cast. The floating line must be straightened so that you have a straight line and leader between rod tip and fly, but as always keep the rod at an angle to the line so that its tip will bear the brunt of a sudden take.

Once you have spotted your rising fish keep as far back from the water edge as possible and take advantage of any natural cover. This may mean getting down to it on one knee if a fish is working a weed-bed in shallow water a few yards out. Your first cast gives the best chance when you are trying for a rising fish and any false casting must be made well away from the target area. In strong ripple and dull light a dark fly is best seen by both fisherman and fish and in medium ripple under dull conditions a size 14 hook will be big enough for most occasions. You can use a larger fly in heavy ripple but keep to smaller sizes in calmer water. Under bright light a light-coloured fly serves best and the hook size must be kept to about size 14 as a maximum. The dry Coch-y-Bonddu or Black Gnat are fine patterns, particularly in conditions of dull light, and a light Sedge pattern or perhaps a Tups Indispensable is as good as most when the fish seem interested in hatching insects of lighter colour in brighter light. A dry Midge will often do the trick when there is a daytime hatch of buzzer and it is apparent that the trout are taking the surface fly as opposed to the pupae.

You must be prepared to watch the feeding habits of the fish which has taken your fancy. It may be that he is lying stationary on the edge of a weed bed taking the hatched fly at fairly regular intervals; alternatively you may have found a cruising fish who is moving fairly fast, sipping the surface insects on a definite line. In the former case you must cast so that your fly drops nicely above the stationary fish and in the latter case the fly should be cast to fall just in front of the advancing fish. If a stationary fish rises to your artificial but refuses it change the fly to one size smaller but keep to the same pattern. If a cruising fish ignores your dry fly which has been placed in readiness for his advance do not move the fly, as he may take it on the return trip if he is moving back and forth on a set line.

A detailed knowledge of entomology is not necessary for successful dry fly fishing from the banks of reservoirs but a little knowledge coupled with careful observation of the available feed which may be found in the marginal waters will often help you to select a deceptive artificial. Dry fly fishing will not suit every reservoir angler. You have to be fascinated by this branch of the sport and may find that you are temperamentally unsuited to it. Under the right conditions of light, ripple and rising fish it can produce very good results but very considerable concentration is required and you must be blessed with keen eyesight so that you can watch that little fly sitting up and wandering about on the water surface.

Under calmer conditions where you have found surface feeding fish you may see small dimples as well as others of much greater size. Do not be misled into thinking that small rings mean small fish. A large trout will take a newly-hatched midge with the utmost delicacy and on the other hand a smaller fish will often create quite a large circle when he decides to rise to a surface fly. If you know a particular spot at your reservoir where you have had good results previously on a dry fly it is always worth a try even if the fish are not showing. Select a dark or light fly depending upon dull or bright conditions, cast out, straighten the line and let the fly sit and wander around in the breeze. Strip off about three yards of spare line and let the fly drift out into the ripple—thus covering a wider area within the window of a deep lying trout. If conditions are calm give the fly a slight tweak every now and again to induce a little life-like movement. For this type of fishing you must be prepared to devote at least ten minutes before deciding that the trout are reluctant to rise on this occasion. Against this, you may cast a dry fly into a quiet bay where no fish are showing and up comes one with a resounding whorl a second after your fly reaches the water. Dry fly fishing can be a most valuable method of searching for fish because if you have a positive response to your first or second cast—even though there may be no signs of fish rising—you know for a certainty you are fishing amongst fish and it will therefore pay to give this spot a good working-over. Casting a dry fly demands the very best and most delicate presentation you can manage. Any clumsy wading or slapping the water during false casting will put rising fish down and ruin the chances of success. Reservoir trout may not be choosy about the type of flies they take when compared with their brothers in the chalk streams, but vibration caused by sloppy wading and bad casting will scare them out of any reasonable range.

Sometimes a trout will swat a fly with his tail before taking it. If this happens when you are fishing a dry fly there is a fair chance that the fish will foul hook his tail into the barb of the fly. If this occurs you can expect fireworks—particularly if it happens to be a rainbow trout who was deceived by your artificial. He will leap and splash around with a fine display of acrobatics in order to free his hooked tail. Once a powerful fish is foul-hooked he can become quite uncontrollable and if you succeed in netting him, congratulate yourself. More often than not the end result is a straightened hook with a little piece of tail gristle lodged in the barb.

Trout will sometimes react to a dry fly in a most unexpected way. Some years ago I was fishing at Chew and had been trying to interest a trout who was persistently rising to hatching insects in a small bay. John was getting his amusement by watching me miss this fish several times and he suggested I might just as well cast my fly into the path of a minnowing trout which he had noticed some twenty yards away from me. I am always prepared to try something new and am well past being insulted on the subject of missing fish, so off I went to apply my dry fly skill to the minnow chaser. I cast out over the line he was working and a few moments later along he came, close to the bank, fast and high in the water, scattering the small fry in his forage. To my amazement he rose and took my dry fly with great precision, and I suggest you try this as an alternative when trying for a minnow chaser who will not respond to the more traditional wet fly tactics.

The timing of a 'strike', or tightening as I prefer to call it, is of vital importance in dry fly fishing. If a fish rolls over your fly, tighten immediately. When a fish makes a little 'hole' in the water he is sucking the dry fly down to him perhaps two or three inches beneath the surface, and when this happens you must give him time before tightening. Where big fish are known to take a dry fly they must be given time to take the fly before tightening. Smaller fish generally snatch and are either on or off in a second. Catching a trout on a dry fly in the dark at the end of a rise results from luck and not skill. On these occasions the trout does the work and suffers for his error. But when the dry fly can be clearly seen by both fisherman and fish, it is the fisherman who must make the decision on the exact timing for a catch. Once a dry fly becomes submerged either during the action of hooking and playing a fish, or perhaps by rough water, it must be dried, re-oiled and blown on to open out the hackles. Watch the fly knot and re-tie it after catching a fish, and as always check the hook barb frequently, particularly if you have risen, pricked and lost a fish. The procedures for playing and landing a fish caught by dry fly tactics are as before but in some cases, particularly where a large rainbow is hooked, the water explodes with his reaction and it is essential to give him line so that he works off his first burst in deep water. Do not let him thrash about on the surface.

To summarize, these reminders for dry fly work will be helpful:

1. The selected dry fly must sit up well on the water.

2. Travel light and explore a lot of likely holding grounds.

3. Use as long a leader as you can handle with as fine a point as you dare.

4. Dull day, dark fly. Bright day, light-coloured fly.

5. Size is more important than colour. Hook sizes of 12 to 14 are generally suitable for daytime fishing but when the light is fading at sunset a size 10 bushy fly will sometimes interest a trout—particularly if there is a hatch of large sedge flies. In conditions of bright light a size 16 midge will often do the trick but it is a risky business using small hooks where the trout are large and powerful.

6. Keep the fly dry. If it is raining give a few brisk short false casts to dry it out. Re-oil frequently and always after catching a fish.

7. Big fish must be given time to take the fly and go down.

8. The bigger the fish the longer the wait before tightening.

9. Follow a bad cast by an immediate retrieve and cast to another direction.

10. If wading is really necessary then get into position as quietly as possible and stay perfectly quiet and still for a few minutes before

Photograph 36. To start a back cast hold the rod handle firmly with your thumb on top. Squeeze the handle and this will tense the forearm muscles. Form a triangle of taut line between the butt ring, reel and line hand. Note that the line hand is held as far down as possible. The triangle of taut line is kept ready for 'shooting' towards the end of the forward cast sequence.

Photograph 37. When retrieving the fly line crook the forefinger of the rod hand over the line against the cork handle. If you suspect an 'offer' to your fly tighten instantly by pinching the line against the handle and raising the forearm simultaneously. In this case the retrieved line is being allowed to fall gradually to the bank, the easiest method to start with — but don't tread on it.

starting to fish. As Isaac Walton wrote many years ago, 'You must study to be quiet'.

The styles of fishing described in this chapter, whether by deep sunk lure, wet fly, nymph or dry fly, will form the basis of our fishing methods throughout the season. In general May, June and early July provide the reservoir bank fisherman with many opportunities for varying his styles of fishing, because during these months the fish are generally on the move at fairly regular intervals throughout the day and particularly so at dawn, sunset and dusk—though I must admit that I am far too lazy to know anything worthwhile about the trout's activity at dawn other than information acquired by reading. There is usually good midday sport during a warm April and May. Towards the end of July and for parts of August the fishing can become a bit dour at times. It seems that the trout do not feed as eagerly during this period, but this is not to say they cannot be deceived into making a mistake by a conscientious fisherman and the next chapter will give a few suggestions for making the best of rather difficult days as well as those which are in the fisherman's favour. More often than not there are good evening rises provided that there is not a sudden fall in air temperature as the sun goes down, and we must look into the possibilities of varied fishing styles which may lead us to a good fish or two at sunset. We must also explore the possibilities of using the leaded nymphs and the Corixa and Shrimper, both of which can lead us to good fish under the right conditions— particularly during September, which is usually a good month for bank fishermen due to the trout's renewed interest in feeding well and getting into prime condition for the long winter ahead, and for spawning. The varied methods of bank fishing for reservoir trout will each lead to success given a fair trial, and you will find that it pays to keep an open mind and adapt your tactics to suit the varying conditions as they occur during the season.

8

Some Chances for Success

This chapter gives some examples of the various opportunities which will present themselves under different seasonal and weather conditions, and suggests suitable tactics for catching your fish. You will need to be mobile and it will pay to carry the bare essentials. You will be using a floating line for most of the time but put a spare reel or spool with a sinking line in your jacket pocket because it may be necessary to change from surface fishing to deep-sunk lure work at fairly short notice. For the purposes of this chapter I am assuming that the cold April and early May days are behind us and that we may look forward to a variety of opportunities of finding trout on the move and feeding in different parts of the reservoir.

Rough water in shallow margins
   For the past ten days there has been a steady breeze rising to moderate wind, blowing off the west bank of the reservoir. Fishermen have been working that bank really hard—they have had the benefit of wind behind them to assist casting and several good catches have been recorded. The popular spots have been really flogged but for the last three days only a few fish have been recorded in the returns. The wind is still westerly and fairly gusty at times. Under these conditions try to find a longish stretch of fairly shallow water on the opposite shore line because by this time there will be no end of foam slicks holding dead and dying fly life, snail and all kinds of feed suspended just on or beneath the surface. More important still, that rough water which has been pounding the eastern bank for ten days or more will have scoured out a variety of the aquatic creatures which the trout devour under these conditions.

It will not be particularly easy or pleasant casting directly into the wind on this shore and there are unlikely to be many fishermen either. This is a case for a floating line and stout leader no more than about 7′ 6″ long made up on the lines suggested in chapter 4. If it is a dullish day a Black and Peacock Spider about size 10 will be fine, but if it is brighter then select a flasher, perhaps a Peter Ross or Dunkeld of perhaps size 10 or 12, and keep to a single fly only in either case. The leader must be well stretched and doused in detergent for full sinking.

The shore line you have selected is about seventy-five yards long and there is shallow water and a reasonable foothold up to six yards out for most of its length. It then shelves down into deeper water. Carefully wade in about three yards or so and then stand so you will be casting approximately parallel to the bank but just a little out of parallel, towards the deeper water. Strip out line—only about ten yards—and proceed to work the entire shore line by a series of short casts and retrieves at varying depths and speeds. Make a methodical search with your fly and then carefully wade on another couple of yards keeping parallel to the shore line. Work the fly from the deep water right back to within a foot or two of the shore line at your side. With any luck you will have a few sharp plucks at the fly and if all goes well you should eventually catch a couple of good fish. This type of fishing is fairly hard work. You have the wind at you and you must keep to short lining to keep the 'belly' out of the line. This belly is the line curve caused by the rough ripple playing against the line tending to drive it in towards the shore. There will probably be trouble with bits of weed at the hook and frequent checking of hook barb and fly knot will be necessary. It will assist casting to make a brisk 'cut-down' on the follow through on the forward cast, and the line shoot must be delayed until the rod is parallel to the water. In this way you will get the least wind resistance to hamper casting. You will be surprised to find how often a good trout may be deceived under these conditions of short line fishing—he is probably working the froth and shallow water taking in the left-overs of previous hatches which have found their way on to this shore, and there will usually be plenty of snail and stickleback to increase his interest.

Keep on the move the whole time: tighten at the slightest sign of a fish anywhere near your fly and be prepared for smash takes.

The fish work these frothy rough water areas very fast and you do not have the chance of a careful watch at the line tip because it is on the move in the rough water the whole time. Keep at it and you should get results. If you do not get any offers change to a weighted Jersey Herd and fish it deeper but with variations in retrieve from very fast to quite slow.

You can try this system during daytime or evening, and although the conditions for fishing may seem a bit unpleasant the main thing to remember is that you are fishing where the fish are likely to be, against fishing where it is more comfortable to cast. If you get good results you will have deserved them. Photograph 38 facing page 128—reproduced from *Still Water Fly Fishing*—shows a stretch of water which would appear to be ideal for this type of short line fishing.

For this type of fishing careful wading is really essential, so that you are able to cast more or less parallel to the shore. My general preference is to avoid wading whenever possible, but for this type of lee-shore fishing, careful and methodical wading is unlikely to set up the type of vibration and fish-scaring which must always be avoided when fishing calmer shallows.

Among the weed beds

As the season moves on established reservoirs usually develop prolific weed beds and these will often cover the greater proportion of some bays which earlier in the season have seemed quite clear and easy to fish. A number of fishermen would take one look at a bay such as that shown in photograph 39 facing page 128, again taken from *Still Water Fly Fishing*, and write off the possibilities of successful fishing. This is far from the case, but again you must adapt your fishing methods to overcome the difficult weed ridden conditions. Certain types of reservoir weed harbour masses of insect life and the trout will work these weed beds with great patience and determination, sometimes lying in no more than a foot or two of water taking in the hatching insects as they emerge. Alternatively they may cruise on a fairly regular pattern along sections of the weed margins and in situations such as these an enterprising bank fisherman may well take a good fish.

In the first place, although the bay looks completely weed-covered have a more careful look and you may probably find an odd channel here and there between patches of weed. Spend a fair while looking for some small break in the marginal weed growth and in particular look for one which has been scoured by an inlet ditch or small feeder stream. Trout will lie out in the weed taking all types of feed brought by the feeder stream, and such a spot must be given a most thorough working-over by the bank fisherman. The floating line should be used with a leader about twelve feet long. If you have a knotless tapered leader with you this is the time to use it, because you will remember that this type of leader is made from extruded monofilament with a gradually decreasing taper from butt to point. There are no knots to collect little bits of weed which impede a very careful slow retrieve.

I suggest you try a size 12 or 14 Ivens Green nymph for a start, and the first method of approach is as follows. Keep back from the water edge and make a neat cast to some point where from previous observation you are fairly sure you will be able to make a very slow retrieve without too much weed obstruction. The smaller-sized hook should travel fairly free of all but thick weed. Ten minutes ago you saw a fish rise very gently with a humping movement just on the far edge of the weed bed, no more than eight yards from the shore. There is another on the same line but to your right. Your fly has been cast into an area where fish appear to be nymphing so keep very still and begin a very slow retrieve in the upper two or three feet of water depth. Bring the nymph in about two inches at a time and just now and again give your rod tip a gentle lift to vary the fishing depth. The line has dipped slightly at the point—tighten! No, that was not a fish but a wisp of weed which tangled the hook and caused the line dip, but you were quite right to react so quickly. Clean the hook, check the barb and make a neat cast into the ten-yard line where occasional nymphing rises are still showing. Another two slow retrieves but still no response. Perhaps you are fishing too deep? These fish are working fairly regularly on the outer weed margin and you must try to get one. Get back on the bank and sit down. Keep quiet and dry your leader. Now grease it from the tip of the floating line to within 6″ of the nymph. Do not change the fly—it has not been refused yet and is as good as any for this type of job. Stretch the leader, and if you have not been using a knotless one remove any bits of weed from the intermediate blood knots, and off you go again. Keep out of the water and cast over that channel which leads out over the weed and into the deeper water. Drop the nymph lightly on the water and straighten the line. You can now see the floating greased leader like a thin pencil on the surface film and your nymph should be about 4″ under the surface. Make a very little retrieve of about an inch or two, just enough to make the nymph wobble. A fish has risen to your nymph and you were only just quick enough to tighten when you saw the dimple made by his rise. He seems firmly hooked and away he bores into deep water; let him go because sooner or later he is going to head back and take cover amongst the weed. Keep your rod high and try to get him to work off his energy in the deeper water, but keep a tight line: If he wants to run again let him run against the reel check, because if you hold him tight that small hook-hold is going to become very weak. This time his run is not quite as powerful. You have a tight line on him, or you did, but now it is going slack. Haul in the slack like mad. Is he still on? Yes—but he has rushed in towards you and taken cover in the weed. You can feel his weight and he is about five yards out lying deep and firmly weeded. What should you do now?

There are three chances which sometimes pay off but in each case there is a firm element of risk. First strip off about three yards of slack line and let it float on the water. If the trout feels the tension removed from the line and leader he may think he is free and eventually swim out of his weed hold into deep water. This move will be reflected immediately by the spare line moving away on the surface and you then have a chance to play him away from the weed and eventually guide him through the channel for netting. If this trick does not work, pay out about six yards of line and lay your rod on the bank. Grasp the line and give a series of firm pulls from one or two directions. These must be gentle but deliberate—it is no good having a tug-of-war when you have a fine point to the leader and a small hook in the opposition. This may move him and if he moves you must look lively and pick up your rod to get him under control again. In the last resort, and only if there are no other fishermen trying the same weed bed who will have their chances completely ruined, find a stone or clod of earth and chuck it into where he is lying. The vibration will scare out your fish, as well as any others who may be feeding, and you can forget about any more fishing in this area for at least an hour or so until the fish return after the shock waves and general commotion die down. Very occasionally a fish will put himself within easy reach of the shore line. If this happens prod the weed with the handle of your landing net and this usually makes him move again. Once a fish has taken cover in this way your efforts to shift him invariably result in a weakened hook hold. If you are lucky enough to land him there is a fair chance that the hook will be damaged, and if this is the case discard it. If it looks all right take it off, cut three inches off the leader point and retie the fly because that last bit of nylon next to the hook eye will have had a good deal of wear during your efforts to free the fish from his cover. In this case you have been lucky because giving the trout slack line paid off after about two minutes. Out he went again and you made a very neat and tidy job of guiding him in for netting in that channel you had in mind when starting to fish this spot.

Two things have been learnt from this bit of fishing. First and most important it was perfectly right to grease the leader so that the nymph was only just under the surface. Previously there had been no offers from the nymphing fish but very shortly after that change of depth and the very gentle wobble imparted to the nymph there was the firm take. So here again depth and presentation proved invaluable, and for most of reservoir fishing this is one of the golden rules for success. The hook size was right, and although the Ivens Green is not tied to represent any particular natural nymph it is a very adequate deceiver for a number of similar occasions. Secondly you learnt a bit about dealing with weeded fish and were lucky in the end, although this is not always the case.

On this occasion you were successful with a nymph just under the surface film. Had you seen the odd fish taking newly-hatched fly off the surface you might have had success with a dry fly cast neatly out over the weed bed and left to wander around about two yards beyond the margin. On a brightish day a dry Midge would have been worth a try but on a dull day a small Black Gnat would have given a better chance for success. The problems of playing and landing would have been the same.

Fishing weed beds at dusk is asking for trouble, but if you are prepared for disappointment as well as good results you may catch the best fish of the day only a few yards out. Sometimes trout will lie in really shallow water, no more than a couple of feet deep, taking hatching sedges as regularly as clockwork. The fish make a sort of sucking noise, and if you are prepared to take a chance cast out a dry sedge at dusk and give it an occasional tweak. You may see a sudden explosion in the water as a large trout realizes that he has made a serious mistake and it is up to you to land him as the light fails and he thrashes about amongst the weeds.

Flat calm

This time we seem to have chosen the wrong day off from work—it was arranged a couple of weeks ago and on arrival at the reservoir the water looks like a mirror. The sunshine is bright and there is not a whisper of breeze. It may be worth a gentle stroll further up the reservoir where there are one or two bays which usually catch a little breeze which creates ripple, so off we go. Unfortunately there is no improvement and we have seen no sign of a fish during the half-hour since we started wandering. Under these conditions of bright sun and flat calm bank fishing is very difficult, but it should not be regarded as hopeless until several approaches have been given a thorough try. It is most probable that any fish within bank casting distance will be lying in deep cooler water and we must use our local knowledge in selecting a spot where the shore line shelves down into deep water. Fortunately there is such a spot a hundred yards up the bank and so we try there. Take out your spare spool or reel with the sinking line and make up a leader about twelve feet long. Tie on a Jersey Herd or perhaps a Black and Peacock Tandem lure. Soak the leader in detergent and wet the lure so that it sinks easily. Make some neat false casts without slapping the water, get out as long a line as you can manage and let it sink completely. This will take a minute or more depending on the sinking qualities of the line and the water depth. When you are sure you have reached bottom start to retrieve very, very slowly and then pause so that the lure rises and falls a little. It is just possible that by a patient series of retrieves in this manner you may get a fish to take interest deep down in this cooler water. It can be a long and rather tedious business, but if you get a fish after working a length of bank in this manner you will have deserved it. If the lure brings no results on a slow deep retrieve then speed up the recovery, but keep deep.

As an alternative, cast out the sinking line and pay out an extra yard or two to form a neat coil about 12" wide, and lay the coil on the bank or across a weed bed so that it cannot sink. Watch the coil and if it starts to unfold tighten immediately, as it is probable that a deep-lying trout has picked up your lure from the bottom and is making off with it. A trout will occasionally pick up a stationary lure, and by tightening at the right moment you may get a good fish.

There is still no sign of a fish moving anywhere, but that stretch of weed a few yards further up is above deep water and perhaps we could try another method there. Change your reel or spool and get back to the floating line. Take out a leader with a dropper about one yard back from the point. Grease the leader as far as the dropper only. Tie a large bushy dry fly on the dropper—make sure it is well doused in floatant and add a small Pheasant Tail nymph to the point. If you have any feelings about purism in your fly fishing you had better not read the next bit because we are going to try out the only form of 'float' fishing permitted by the reservoir regulations. Keep on the bank and make a neat and tidy cast over the weed so that the large dry fly sits like a small duckling on the water surface. The small nymph will be suspended about two feet beneath the dry fly. You will remember that this is a leaded pattern and it sinks readily until restrained by the large floating fly. The theory here is that we hope there may be the odd fish lying in deeper water outside the weed and we are going to try and make him interested in that little nymph which he may see in his window from the depths. Straighten the floating line and give the dry fly a little tweak. This is not a retrieve but just a slight careful jerk on the fly line. By tweaking the dry fly you will make the nymph wobble beneath, and a series of such movements may arouse interest in a deep-lying fish who might decide to take the slowly-moving nymph. If you see the slightest dip or unusual movement in the dry fly which is acting as your 'float' then tighten immediately. If you tighten into a fish under these conditions all kinds of problems will arise before landing him among the weed. However, we have looked into various ways of trying to overcome these and you must do your best to apply your knowledge in getting the fish into your landing net. Provided you have patience this system can bring you the occasional fish, so give it a fair trial. Just once in a while you will have the shock of your life when a trout appears from nowhere and decides to take the ridiculous large dry fly instead of the nymph, so be prepared for this because in reservoir fishing the most unexpected things happen fairly often. When you tighten into a fish under these conditions it is more than an even chance that either the dry fly or nymph will get caught up in the weed while you are trying to land your fish. If he has taken the dry fly there is some hope because the small hook of the nymph may soon become clogged by weed and in this way may not offer much obstruction if it brushes against other weed. On the other hand if the fish takes the small nymph, as intended, there is a considerable chance that the larger hook of the dry fly will become entangled. If this happens you must try to get the leader as near to you as possible and cut the dry fly off with your scissors. This will involve wading amongst weed and general mucking-about including the loss of the large fly. In short, two flies near weed nearly always cause trouble, but just occasionally this type of 'float' fishing will relieve a dull spell and if all goes really well you may have a well-earned fish and be left with your two flies and leader intact. When fishing amongst weed beds have the leader point on the heavy side to give some safety margin against a break if it becomes necessary to remove a fish who has taken cover in weed after being hooked.

This 'float' and nymph method can often produce really good results if the dry fly and nymph can be cast into ripple, because the ripple will make the dry fly bobble about and this will cause the nymph to move about beneath with a life-like movement. Unfortunately we have no ripple today—so what else can we do?

One of my favourite approaches during flat calm is the use of the leaded nymph. Again deep water must be sought within bank casting range and you keep to the floating line. Select the longest leader in your box, preferably fifteen feet of it, and soak it with the detergent pad. Stretch it thoroughly and tie on a single leaded nymph at the point—perhaps Sawyer's Grayling Lure or Grey Goose. Keep on the bank and put out as long a line as you can manage without surface disturbance. Mend the line and allow at least a minute or more for the leaded nymph to sink completely. Make sure your floating line is straight and keep your rod tip down, but as always at an angle to the line. Now start a series of slow and gentle rod tip lifts of about two or three feet at a time, then lower the rod tip and gather in the slack line. This lift and retrieve will cause the leaded nymph to rise and fall very slowly in the deeper water. Watch the point at which the floating line tip meets the leader and if there is the slightest deflection, dip, draw or other suspicious movement tighten immediately. This method of leaded nymph fishing demands considerable concentration and you will be amazed to find how a large fish will sometimes be induced to take the slowly-moving artificial and above all with such little disturbance of the floating line tip at the surface. If the leaded nymph does not produce anything after a while, then change to a deeply sunk Worm Fly or other favourite lure and repeat the same slow and methodical tactics. There may not be the slightest sign of a surface feeding fish for as far as you can see, but even under flat calm conditions there are usually several skulking around in the deeps and it is up to you to deceive them. It is not easy work and you must not expect to be successful too often—but these are methods by which trout may be caught and each method has occasionally worked for me during these difficult conditions.

Sometimes during flat calm, particularly towards evening, just when you are hoping for a little ripple and the beginning of an evening rise, the air chills and mist gradually rolls across the water. This starts with wisps and later accumulates into a thickish damp blanket. When this rolling mist arrives with its consequent lowering of surface temperature at the end of a hot day, I have yet to find any method which will lead me to catching a trout. I have tried every form of fishing from sunk lure upwards but can never recall catching anything. There must be an answer somewhere but I am convinced that rolling mists after flat calm are the most hopeless conditions for reservoir fishing, and when they arrive I pack up.

Shallow bays

In very hot weather at the peak of summer, trout will seldom be found in shallow water of about three feet or less due to the high water temperature and lack of oxygen, but during the middle of May when the water first warms and the insect life is livening up, and again towards September when the shallows are cooling, there are tremendous opportunities for trout fishing—provided always that the shallows have not been ruined by careless wading with consequent fish scaring. You may have to walk a long way but there are great opportunities in quiet shallow bays and they must be explored fully. In the first place, if you are interested in learning a little about insect life it is well worth having a poke around here and there at the margins. Lift up the odd stone and you may find water leeches. You may also find fresh water shrimp, little black snails, stickleback and most probably blood worms and above all the water boatmen or Corixa, all of which form part of the trout's diet.

A small magnifier such as the one mentioned when dealing with equipment etc. will give you a really good enlarged picture of these creatures. As another aid towards research, quite apart from the value and wisdom of wearing polaroid glasses to shield your eyes from the glare off bright water, you can obtain most useful knowledge of underwater conditions by using these glasses to peer down close to the water surface into the deeps and shallows, amongst the weeds and into the rocky parts. By seeing into such waters through polaroids you are able to appreciate the sort of snags you may encounter when fishing and retrieving in a particular spot, and above all, by keeping dead still for a while it is occasionally possible to see a trout or two lurking around amongst his native surroundings.

The occasional hour or two spent on periodic research of this kind will certainly add considerably to your enjoyment of reservoir fishing because you will get an idea of the type of creatures you must try to imitate under different fishing conditions, and of suitable matching artificials to complete the deception. Look at those water snails and then soak a small Black and Peacock Spider and compare the two. That blood worm looks remarkably like the artificial Buzzer Red Larva—and the Shrimper looks a pretty fair match for the freshwater shrimp you found amongst the stones. Now look at those little water boatmen and see how they match up with the Corixa patterns in your box. The small Pheasant Tail nymph could be matched to the water boatmen as well. Many expert fly fishermen have spent years studying aquatic and land-bred creatures of interest to the trout, and whilst for the greater part of reservoir fishing exact imitations are not important there are some occasions where a fair imitation will definitely give good results, and shallow bays probably offer some of the best opportunities for this type of bank fishing.

Here is a story to illustrate the point. In September 1970 I was to meet my friend John Burgess for a day or two at Blagdon. The fishing had been poor from both bank and boat for several days and it seemed that once again I had picked the wrong time for a short fishing holiday. Before meeting at the fishing lodge we had planned to fish the long exposed shallow northern shore, but during the night the wind had gone right round and the morning greeted us with a blustery south wind, drizzle and the occasional spot of sunshine lasting for about ten minutes at each interval. John knows every inch of Blagdon shore line, and on his advice we left the car at Green Lawn and set forth to a small bay about three hundred yards east of Rainbow Point. No-one else was there and judging by the lack of footprints in the low muddy shore line no-one had been bank fishing recently. We stood back about twenty yards to see if there were any signs of fish. During the next ten minutes or so two trout showed their tails no more than a yard from the water edge. John remarked that they might be taking snail or Corixa, stirring up the mud to sort them out. This diagnosis made good sense because the previous night I was talking to a chap in the bar of the 'Live and Let Live' (the pub of all pubs in Blagdon) and he told me he had spooned two fish taken that day in the shallows of Home Bay and both were stuffed with Corixa, snail and blood worms.

I will not go into the full details of the rest of our day at that little bay except to say that John took a limit bag of eight fine trout out of the shallow water and at the end of it all he had not waded above his knee caps. Six fish were taken on Corixa patterns of small size (12 or 14) of different colours, one on a small Jersey Herd and the last at dusk on a Worm Fly. Floating line tactics were used and the Corixa patterns were fished very gently at varying depths with a slight jerky retrieve plus a little rod top lift to give animation. The Jersey Herd came into its own when the Corixa ceased to interest the trout and the Worm Fly is one of the most reliable takers at Blagdon when fish are on the move. When the fish were opened up they were all found to be stuffed with water boatmen and the Corixa patterns had proved themselves to be the most valuable deceivers.

There are several points worth noting from that little story:

1. The value of knowing where fish are likely to be on a particular reservoir under certain weather conditions and at a given time in the season.

2. The importance of assessing the type of feed having regard to the rise form.

3. The tactics which led to six fish being deceived by a reasonable imitation of the natural creatures in the shallow water.

4. The avoidance of wading during fishing, thus leaving the shallow bay as undisturbed as possible.

5. The value of the Jersey Herd and Worm Fly as general attractors despite the trouts' preoccupation with natural feed.

Just as we did a little 'float' fishing during the flat calm in deep water, try these 'ledger' tactics in a shallow bay. Keep to a floating

line, and use a twelve-foot leader with a single dropper three feet
back from the point. Tie a leaded Grayling Lure on the point and a
small Black and Peacock Spider on the dropper. Cast out and let the
leader sink fully. Straighten the line and shortly you should have the
leaded point nymph resting on the bottom with the buoyant Black
and Peacock swaying attractively above it. Keep the fly line still and
watch the point at which the line and leader meet the water. If a
fish takes the Black and Peacock during his search for feed you will
have a perfect signal at the line tip. This is a good trick and is well
worth trying in shallow water. The leaded nymph must lie on the
bottom to achieve the right conditions. The Shrimper must always
be given a fair try in shallow bays—particularly where there is a
stony bottom and even more so if you have found signs of fresh
water shrimp during that little bit of research you decided to do
when things were rather quiet. Keep to a twelve-foot leader and
fish the Shrimper by rod top lift to vary the depths. Alternatively
fish it very slowly along the stony bottom with a series of little
jerks.

It is impossible to over-emphasize the value of shallow water when
bank fishing for reservoir trout, and it should be preserved by the
avoidance of unnecessary wading and clumsy fishing methods so
that the trout are encouraged into and not scared away from these
valuable feeding grounds. You may have to walk a long way to find
the type of shallow margins as shown in photograph 2 facing page 16,
but if you work hard and concentrate you may well find and eventually catch trout of three pounds and up feeding hard and regularly
in no more than three or four feet of water. The rainbow trout in
photograph 40 facing page 129 was a fine cock fish of 4 lb 2 oz and
only 20½" long. I first saw him cruising and tailing in a stretch of
weed about five yards off the eastern shore at Bough Beech during
an evening's fishing in September 1971. I fished for him at the same
position with lures, nymphs, dry and wet flies during three early
morning and three evening sessions and on the third evening in flat
calm and fading light I decided the time had come when traditional
tactics must be abandoned. I greased a Worm Fly and cast it two
yards beyond his favourite patch of weed. After giving the lure a
couple of tweaks there was an explosive take followed by a series
of nerve-racking runs. I netted him eventually but why this fish
should snatch at a ridiculous floating Worm Fly I shall never know.

Perseverance and luck play a considerable part in this type of bank fishing, particularly when as in this case the fish was found to be stuffed with stickleback.

A good evening rise

Let's assume that all conditions are right for a really good evening rise. The sun is going down, you know the water well and the wind is dropping to a mild whisper just sufficient to keep a ripple on the water. Before you start off make a routine check through your jacket pockets so you know where each item of tackle is. For perhaps two hours you are going to be fishing constantly to fish on the move and showing at regular intervals. This will be the time for the floating line and greased leader, but apart from your usual spare leaders have one specially soaked in detergent, about twelve feet long; you will need this leader during the last half hour or so before it's time to pack up fishing. You have walked a long way up the bank to one of your favourite spots and the nearest bank fisherman is about forty yards away. At this particular spot you are within easy casting distance of the ripple edge of a 'calm lane', which in this case is running parallel to your shore. You will remember my earlier reference to the importance of calm lanes to the reservoir fisherman, due mainly to their encouraging insect hatches in the calmer air which lies above the calm water and to the trout's instinct to cruise or remain almost stationary in the length of a lane feeding upon the insects which frequently hatch under these favourable conditions.

You recognize that chap out in the boat about fifty yards from the shore. He knows his stuff and will not drift inshore towards you, nor will he bang the oars about in the rowlocks scaring the fish out of your range or his. Check your foothold along the shoreline you have chosen, it will be dark when you pack up and it is not funny dragging yourself out of soft heavy mud. You have chosen the west bank, which means the sun will be off the water sooner than the opposite side of the lake and things will probably start happening any moment now. You remember that clump of reeds about thirty yards to your right, where you lost a good rainbow when he went to weed two weeks ago. Since that accident one of your fishing pals has told you how to put on side strain to prevent a powerful fish from having his way. This involves the use of the rod at an angle with the butt pointing towards the fish. The full power of the rod is developed and by maintaining this pressure you turn him out towards your front.

It is probable that a variety of insects will be hatching during this particular evening and so here are a few suggestions which may lead to success for each kind.

Sedge

As you watch the water, two tiny dimples have shown five yards from the bank and two perfect sedge flies are just preparing for 'lift-off'. They are soon airborne and a fish rises about eight yards out. Other fish are showing every two minutes or so and sedge are now hatching in fair numbers. Under these conditions I suggest you start as follows.

Select a twelve-foot leader with a spare dropper link about three feet back from the point. Grease the leader and stretch it thoroughly. The spare dropper link will be used later on. Tie on a dry Sedge to the leader point, similar in size and colour to the naturals which are hatching. Make a point of soaking dry flies in floatant well before fishing starts, as this gives them plenty of time to dry out. Like this they will fish for an evening without further treatment unless drowned by a fish which you have caught, when a fresh dressing of floatant will of course be required. Do not wade in. Keep about two yards back from the water and try a neat and accurate cast to cover the next fish that rises. If the dry fly is refused or produces no result after covering half a dozen rises it is pretty obvious that the trout are not taking a fully-hatched insect or perhaps they do not like your pattern. Do not waste any further time. The sedge are still hatching. Take off the dry fly and tie on a Sedge Pupa or an Ivens Brown nymph. Give the end of the leader a thorough wiping with your detergent pad to remove the grease from the last 6" of the leader up to the fly. Cast out, and straighten the line and leader immediately. Watch the joint between line and leader and retrieve in the slowest possible manner about an inch at a time. The artificial will then be 'hanging' about four inches under the surface and the ripple which is still there will give a little wobbly life to the fly. Keep perfectly still and con-centrate on that leader, which should show up like a pencil line passing through the ripple. You notice a slight draw and deflection in the leader. Tighten immediately and you have him. The fish bores down fast and into the deep water which shelves about twenty

Photograph 38. Sometimes the fish are in the surf on the lee shore. The bank fisherman must adapt his casting and fishing tactics to take advantage of such conditions even though it may be more comfortable to cast from the opposite bank with the wind behind him. Tactics for lee-shore fishing are outlined in chapter 8 under the sub-heading 'Rough water in shallow margins'.

Photograph 39. Never regard a heavily weeded bay as hopeless for bank fishing. It will be difficult to fish but most probably there will be fish feeding regularly amongst the weed beds and you must adapt your tactics to deceive them. Suggestions for doing so are included in chapter 8 under the sub-heading 'Among the weed beds'. Both photographs on this page have been reproduced from *Still Water Fly Fishing* by kind permission of T. C. Ivens.

Above: Photograph 40. This rainbow was only 20½" long but weighed 4 lb 2 oz. You can see it is a cock fish by the protruding bottom jaw. Although stuffed with stickleback, he became enraged and snatched at a Worm Fly greased to float and tweaked just off his favourite patch of weed. Unusual tactics sometimes pay good dividends in reservoir fishing.

Below: Photograph 41. A rainbow of 2 lb 4 oz and 15" long. A hen fish, easily recognized by the receding lower jaw and relatively shorter head. She seized a Jersey Herd in the fading light of 30th September 1971 – the end of the season for both of us.

yards out. There is no surface leaping or general acrobatics which generally occur when a rainbow is hooked and this one is probably a useful brown trout. Fortunately he does not give too much trouble, you have him under control and after about three minutes decide he is ready for the net. At this point you can wade into the water, very gently to avoid any more disturbance than need be. Submerge your net completely and draw the fish over. In he topples to the bottom of the deep net—a fine brownie of about 1¾ lb. Move back out of the water quietly, get back up the bank on to firm ground and kill your fish instantly. Slide him into the polythene bag. Do not waste time congratulating yourself, the light is fading and the fish are still feeding and moving fast. Make a careful check of the hook barb and fly knot to see that it is still sound. Wipe your hands on the piece of rag in your pocket so that you do not get any fish slime onto the tip of your floating line, because it will make it sink. Dry and re-grease the leader and repeat the performance which has just led to success. Vary the direction of cast over an arc to cover different parts of the water, and keep to a slow retrieve.

Three casts later you are watching your leader and suddenly the water explodes. The line tightens and a rainbow leaps two or three times and starts tearing across the water doing a sort of half-skate and half-swim. Let him run but get well back and move up the bank to get a tight line on him. Keep your rod tip as high as possible, but if he jumps lower it momentarily to give just a little slack which may prevent a break. Try and remember this rule—it is very important.

You have now regained the line and fish, and leader, line, rod, reel and you are all together. He still wants to run and is making for that weed bed over on the right. Put on side strain gradually but with determination and slowly turn him back into the deeper water. This is a good fish and he is going to weaken the hook hold at every run, so you decide that the time has come to put on the pressure. Do this very gradually by reeling in against the power of the fish and keep the butt of your rod vertical so that the whole rod can flex against each move of the fish. House the rod handle firmly to your navel. He seems to be tiring, so reel him in to within five yards. Be patient. Keep the pressure on him and remember that generations of knowledge have been applied to the design of that small hook, to say nothing of the skill of the man who built your rod. You can feel every fibre of it working right through to the butt. Reel in very slowly and now you see that the joint between fly line and leader has just gone through the top ring. Carefully submerge your net beneath the water and draw in the fish by deliberate pressure on the rod in a backward movement over your right shoulder. The fish rolls on his side. Very slowly draw him over the fully submerged net, make a clean job of it and for heaven's sake do not let him use his last energy in getting purchase on the net frame with his tail as you raise the net to receive him. If he does this he may gather sufficient strength for a backward leap and you will lose him for certain. He topples into the deep net and back you go up the bank to complete last rites without delay or fuss. A fine rainbow of three pounds plus, with a small head, deep powerful body and brilliant silvery purple sheen—a cock fish in prime condition.

That rainbow trout created a great deal of surface disturbance and it is more than likely that other fish have been scared off while you have been bringing him to the net. Remember that trout are tremendously sensitive to vibration, and the shock waves caused by a powerful fish are very likely to alarm other fish in the vicinity. Under these circumstances move about thirty yards further up the bank to undisturbed water. You will have to risk the new foothold in the fading light. Take off that small fly but do not put it back with your good ones. Put it in a match box in your trouser pocket so that you can check the hook and barb in detail tomorrow and then cut off 6" from the point of the leader. Both fly and leader point have done their fair share of this evening's work and it will be wise to tie your next fly to the reduced leader point.

Caenis

The wind has dropped and the ripple has gone. From nowhere there have suddenly appeared clouds of little grey and white flies. They swarm all round clinging to your jacket, and crawling into your ears and over your hands. Some settle on the rod, others lie in the rod rings and even on the spare coils of fly line. These little characters are named Caenis and with some justification have been awarded the title 'fishermen's curse'.

When trout are feeding during a Caenis hatch they cruise in a completely leisurely fashion and seem to become totally absorbed in their feeding. They become oblivious of fishermen, fly lines, leaders and artificial flies. Once at Blagdon during a Caenis rise I had a large brown trout cruising up and down just off the north shore with my leader across its dorsal fin. It made no objection at all to this arrangement for half a minute or more during which time it sipped up hundreds of these tiny flies floating in the surface film. The fish are right at the water surface during this activity and both dorsal and tail fins show frequently.

When this type of very selective feed is on some fishermen advocate:

1. A very small dry fly such as the Grey Duster or Last Hope, both of which are tied to match the general size and pattern of the natural. By very small I mean about size 18.

2. Fishing beneath the surface with your favourite wet fly, working on the principle that where fish are showing on the surface others are generally beneath.

3. Casting out a large black and heavily-hackled dry fly tied to a greased leader. This large fly is tweaked occasionally in the hope that the cruising fish will take it for a change.

4. Packing up and going to the nearest pub.

I have had limited success with methods 2 and 3 and regard 4 as the logical conclusion to any fishing trip.

It is a very difficult rise to fish and I can say no more. One thing I have learned about Caenis will stick in my mind for ever. Several years ago I was fishing the north shore at Weir Wood up past the first shelter when there was a tremendous rise to Caenis. Brown trout were sipping them up and cruising round and round in small circles moving no more than three to four yards from the bank. One fish eventually moved so slowly and close that I netted him during this leisurely feed. I thought the fish was either blind, sick or both. I took him up on the bank to discover that he was completely and utterly gorged with these insects. His mouth was packed solid with drowned Caenis, there was not room for one more and his jaws were jammed open. If this happens to one fish presumably others must become similarly stuffed and slow-witted and perhaps this throws a little light on why it is so difficult to catch trout when Caenis are on the water.

Buzzers

I have previously emphasized how important these insects are to the reservoir trout and there is usually a buzzer hatch during a good

evening rise. You are now well into dusk and the fish start rising
with a peculiar 'plop' noise, first well out in deep water and shortly
afterwards closer towards the shore. The air becomes filled with a
humming noise and you notice the insects suspended with their
hooked bodies almost permanently poised in the warm still air. Try
a black Buzzer on the point, and you will remember that we tied
on a spare dropper which has not been used yet. A Footballer Size 14
will be a useful fly to tie on here. The last 4″ of the leader point has
been well soaked in detergent, likewise the dropper link, but the
remainder of the leader is carefully greased. Keep on the bank and
cast out about fifteen yards. Straighten the line and leader immediately. The heavier Buzzer on the point will be about 3″ below
the surface film and the smaller Footballer dropper should hang just
beneath the surface. Make a very careful retrieve so slowly that the
nymphs only just wobble. It is now too dark to watch the joint
between line and leader for any signs of a take. The answer here is
to make a small loop of slack line between the rod point and water,
keeping the rod tip as close to the water as possible but always at an
angle to the fly line as previously recommended. Watch this little
loop of slack line and at the slightest movement tighten. It usually
works. If Sedge and Buzzers are both hatching at the same time it
usually pays to concentrate upon Buzzer tactics and not the Sedge.

The grand finale

After a good evening rise of the type outlined it seems that
suddenly, as if a referee has blown the whistle, all fish go down. It
is dark, calm and less than half an hour before packing up time.
Take out your small torch, pointing any light down towards the
bank and shielded from the water by your body. Take off the greased
leader. Leave the flies tied on and put it away somewhere safe. You
can sort that out tomorrow. Time is precious. Take out the spare
leader which was previously soaked with the detergent pad and tie
on either a Worm Fly, a large Black and Peacock Spider or your
favourite lure. Give the leader a good stretch, check the line and
fly knots twice. With any luck you may get the best fish of the
evening during the next twenty minutes. It seems that after all
surface activity has died down and the light has gone completely
larger fish move right in, probably with the idea of gorging the
stickleback and insects which are now gradually sinking from the sur-

face film towards the bed. You can risk fishing a large wet fly or lure
now and preferably one whose silhouette is going to stand out well
in the dark. Cast out about twelve yards with the floating line and
avoid wading if possible. Straighten the fly line quietly and then
allow several seconds for the leader to sink. Avoid surface disturbance and work your fly in short jerks using rod top lift to help vary
the depth of the fly. Be prepared for a smash take and in particular
be very careful on the point of lift-off as you are about to make a
back cast, because frequently a large trout will follow a lure right
to the surface before deciding to take it, and when this happens and
you are unprepared, a break is usually a certainty. If there has been
a prolific hatch of Sedge earlier in the evening a Worm Fly fished in
this manner can be really deadly. As an alternative to the deeply
sunk fly during this late period here is another system. Instead of
removing the greased leader which has given success earlier in the
evening snip off 6" from the point and tie on the largest bushy dry
fly you have in your box, having previously doused it in floatant
so that it sits on the water like a small haystack. Cast out about
twelve to fifteen yards and straighten the floating line. Keep the
index finger of your rod hand lightly over the line in the normal
manner and strip the line back as fast as you can in a continuous
retrieve to make the huge dry fly 'skate' across the surface. Do this
in a continuous movement and be prepared for fireworks if a good
fish decides to ignore the disturbance and snatch at the fly. It is
possible to use the Worm Fly well soaked with floatant for this job.
Any fish who is prepared to ignore the surface film disturbance to
this extent is not going to be choosy about the tying of the fly which
has aroused his senses at this late hour of the evening. If you are
successful with either of these late hour tactics and have been working from a gentle shore line it is probably better to play out a good
fish and beach him rather than to fumble around with the landing
net in the dark. Beaching a fish is fairly safe when he is firmly hooked
with a large fly—you must be sure to play him out in deep water and
when he tires bring him into the shore in a continuous firm movement making sure to keep his head just above the surface and above
all, steer clear of heavy weed and similar snags which will prevent
a clean landing.

    If you succeed in catching a trout during the last few minutes of
an evening rise you will quite often find he is in prime condition.

Open him carefully when you get home—you will probably find him stuffed with midge pupae, corixa, snail, blood worms, bits of stickleback and the remains of all kinds of fly life. Quite often when making the last cast or two before packing up you will be shattered by an almighty take, the like of which you have never felt before. This is probably from a really big fish who has been following your lure or largish wet fly and who is enraged at its continual movement. More often than not fish and fishermen part company fairly rapidly when this occurs late at night, but if you are ready for him and have a bit of luck you may catch the trout of a season.

You must realize that although fly fishermen look forward to catching a good trout during an evening rise there are many occasions when it seems no matter how hard you try, the fish ignore your flies completely. This is probably due to the fact that the trout are preoccupied on one type of hatching insect, and unless you happen to have an artificial of the same size fished at the exact taking depth, no matter how carefully you fish you may not get the desired result; on the other hand, there is usually a good chance of catching a trout just before the main rise starts and again just after it has died down. As T. C. Ivens reminds us in his *Still Water Fly Fishing*, 'an evening rise is never dull, merely gloriously infuriating'.

In this chapter we have seen various methods available for fishing under differing seasonal conditions—each one has given me a lot of enjoyment and some measure of success. No doubt there are other ways to be explored for each occasion, and this is all to the good because with reservoir fishing it seems there is something new to be learnt all the time.

9

The Unexpected

Bank fishermen suffer accidents and misfortunes just as all others who follow their chosen sport. The beginner is particularly vulnerable, but even the more experienced seem to have their off days when nothing goes right during a day's fishing. In this chapter it may be helpful to set out the sort of things that can go wrong and to offer suggestions for remedial action in each case. I have experienced each accident and situation under review and doubtless there will be others in store, but here are some events which are pretty certain to occur, and some advice as to what to do.

Shipping water

You have decided to wade in. The water is very rough with a heavy lop like a mild sea. The wind is behind and the bottom provides a firm foothold. You wade out until the water is just above your knees and start to get out line. Your casting is quite good but you think another five yards would be useful. You wade in further until the water is up to your thighs. Fine—there is another six inches or so between water level and your wader tops. You are enjoying the fishing—that forward cast is fairly sizzling out. The winds seems to be getting up. How right you are. Just then a strong wave slaps your backside and you feel the water running into the back of your waders and down towards your feet.

You did not pay enough attention to the lop of the water surface in relation to the top of your waders. This would not have mattered had you been wearing trouser waders, but for safety reasons these are usually prohibited in reservoir fishing. Back you go to the bank, slop, slop, slop, each wader holding a pint of water. What's to be done now? You have two alternatives. Either empty out and carry on fishing in cold sodden socks and trousers—not much pleasure—or better still walk back to the car where you have a spare pair of thick socks. Put them on and cover each dry sock with a polythene bag. Now you can resume fishing with dry feet. The polythene bag will stop the fresh socks getting wet from the sodden waders, but when you get home stuff the waders with dry newspaper and hang them upside down in a warm room to dry out. A spare pair of thick socks and several polythene bags are most useful items in any fisherman's car. The polythene acts as an insulator and will keep your feet warm under the worst conditions.

Falling in

This is not funny and regrettably there have been fatal accidents. The worst conditions are in treacherous soft mud. I first fell in at Blagdon near the dam in Pipe Bay. Fish were rising right in the corner of the dam and in my enthusiasm for reaching them I did not pay enough attention to the very soft muddy margin. Down went one wader but my other foot was on firm ground. I had no chance because the suction from the soft mud was greater than my strength to resume a vertical position. My immediate thought was 'keep the rod up'. This I did and fell gracefully sideways into the lot. The rod was saved. I was completely immersed in soft muddy water.

On another occasion at Darwell I was foolish enough to get into what appeared to be firm silt but which was in fact treacherous loose mud. This time I stood with both waders sinking evenly—rather like going down in a slow moving lift. I decided the only thing to do was to fall gracefully backwards, again holding the rod tip as high as possible to prevent a break. By falling slowly back I was gradually able to draw each foot out of the half submerged wader. I had to paddle back to firm ground and return with a couple of fence pales to make a standing for the wader recovery. The lack of footprints at my chosen fishing spot should have aroused some suspicion. Getting stuck in soft mud can be very dangerous indeed. The physical exertion of trying to get out can be tremendous. Always be suspicious of attractive looking spots without give-away footprints. Try each step for firmness very carefully. If you find a shallow bay with dry mud and weed around, be extremely cautious. Look for gravelly sections amongst the mud—these are usually firmer. If you intend to return to such a bay at dusk mark your way in and out with a few twigs or reeds stuck in at intervals. Never fish off a slimy dam or rocky margin unless you have studded waders. Rubber-soled waders are lethal under the slippery conditions which form when wet weed clings to rock or concrete. If you see a fisherman badly stuck in the mud tell him to stay put with the minimum of exertion. This is no time for mucking about. Planks and rope may be needed in the shortest possible time, so look lively and get help with the minimum delay. Always be very careful when fishing from a bank which is being eroded by deep water lashing against its face. Eventually the bank subsoil will give way, and if you are on the turf above, you will go with it. Reservoirs with deep water right up to the margins can frequently provide this hazard. Remember also that wet clay shrinks rapidly under hot sun, and a section of shore which has been sound when the clay remains wet will rapidly become friable after a hot dry spell, which will cause evaporation of subsoil moisture.

If you are away for a few days or even a long day's fishing a spare shirt and the largest old jersey in the back of the car will be the greatest comfort if you have a really unfortunate accident of this kind. No one wants to go about prepared for the worst but a couple of really warm dry garments of some kind can always be left in the car and may save you a very wet, miserable and dangerously cold journey back to home or wherever else you may be staying.

Fly in the face

This again is not funny. When casting in heavy wind it always pays to put your jacket hood up whether it is raining or not. If you make a bad cast and the fly, or flies, clout the back of your hood no damage is done. If you wear goggles or a sun visor the chances of damage to the eyes are negligible. If you get a fly in the face, neck or ear you will know instantly whether the barb has gone in, and the first thing to do is to cut the nylon and leave the damned thing where it has stuck. Pack up and walk to the nearest fisherman. He may be able to remove the fly by a careful movement or a nick of the skin with a razor blade. Let the cut bleed freely.

If you have a fly hook badly stuck near your eye or lips some professional attention is the first essential. You will feel wretchedly embarrassed and a fair amount of pain, but in order to avoid any permanent damage and infection a doctor's help is needed. Fortunately a lot of doctors take up fly fishing and they are usually very good at it, probably because they are naturally interested in the ento-mological side. The bailiff may know if one of his doctor fishermen is at the reservoir when you get to the fishing hut for help. If there is you are very lucky, but if not, be sensible and go off for the nearest medical treatment available without any further delay.

Missing two in succession

You are watching the tip of your floating line. It dips, you tighten and the fish is on, only for a few seconds, after which the line goes slack and you feel a bit lost. You cast again, three retrieves later another good take, the beginnings of a first rush, a first leap and again the line goes slack. You are now convinced that you will never be any good at this game and feel utterly depressed. Instead of sitting there doing nothing have a look at that fly. Exactly, the barb is miss-ing! You should have checked it before you cast to the first fish, never mind the second. Then you remember an earlier bad back cast when you hit some reeds behind. It was probably then that the barb went. Keep checking your flies constantly during fishing, and always when a trout is lost.

Missing two more in succession

A sudden take by a really powerful fish—three leaps and a fine rainbow tears out line in a tremendous rush. Perhaps this is the biggest fish you have hooked. Your rod is up high and you are in contact with the fish. Another tremendous run follows which takes out the rest of your line and most of your backing. You see the fish make yet another leap sixty yards away and still you are in contact— you have moved back up the bank to try to keep a tight line. After a battle of about two minutes the whole line goes completely slack. Haul in like mad—he may be rushing in towards you. You see the same fish leap five yards away from the bank, the line is pathetically slack, yards of it on the shore and the rest in the water. This is the old problem we have looked at before: a really powerful fish who turned inshore at tremendous speed and by lashing and writhing against the slack line has freed himself. The whole thing happens in seconds—a large rainbow will travel like a rocket under these con-ditions, and despite the frantic hauling of loose line as he rushed at you it still was not fast enough. A reel with an automatic retrieve lever would most probably have coped with this situation but we are still using the traditional fly reel. Two nearby fishermen had the courtesy to stop fishing and get out of the water when they saw your fish sixty yards out—they knew you were into a really fine fish and if he made contact with either of their lines your chances of success would have been hopeless. That was very bad luck indeed, you lost a beauty.

Reel the backing carefully through, check the line splice, and reel the line evenly onto your reel. Check the leader. Cut off, check and re-tie the fly just to make sure. See if you can get another to take. There seem to be big fish in this spot. That fish took your fly savagely and with tremendous power. Three casts later you are taken again, two, three, and two more leaps from another good rainbow, he wants to run but you are determined to keep this one at close quarters. The rod is flexing violently but you hold him. The fish is thrashing about on the surface only fifteen yards away. You feel his powerful movements and fast side-swims on the short line. Still you hold him and then all goes slack and you know you have lost another. That was not bad luck—it was plain very bad fishing. You knew your fly and leader were good and you were determined not to lose that second fish, but you cannot hold a powerful rainbow or brown trout on a short line like that. Every fresh wrench by the fish is loosening the hook hold against your tight handling and eventually the hold gave. No, the hook is still on the leader with a bit of gristle in the bend. You lost the first fish through very bad luck when there was an uncontrollable rush by a big fish towards you, but you lost the second because you had previously made up your mind that the next fish was not going to be allowed any long runs. He had different ideas and the strength to fulfil them in his bid for freedom. The time to put on the pressure comes after a powerful fish has been allowed perhaps two or three runs. Holding a fish on a short line and allowing it to thrash about on the water surface at the beginning of a fight is very bad fishing indeed.

Two at a time

This time you have mounted two flies on the leader and are doing a little nymph fishing in the shallows. A sudden take and another a second later. You are now in the happy position of having one fish on the point and another on the dropper. They are fighting you and each other. Keep calm and let them fight it out well below the water surface. Keep back, let them run against the reel check and gradually put on the pressure. There are several schools of thought about landing two on the same leader but it generally pays to net first the fish which has taken the point fly. If you manage this and have a deep net you may be able to guide the second fish into the net without too much trouble. If you lose the second at least one is safe.

The forgotten landing net

You have finished your lunch and now decide to move round to the next bay. It is a fine day for fishing and you have two in the bag. You walk confidently to the next bay, check the leader and fly and after two or three neat false casts out goes your line. Twenty minutes later you are taken deep and firmly, no surface commotion this time, just a steady deep run and some powerful rod flexing. This seems to be a really good brown trout and he has been deceived by your Ivens Green nymph. You play the fish well and have a feeling of confidence that at long last you really are beginning to get the idea. Now for the landing net. No—it is no good feeling for the net clip because that net is one hundred and fifty yards away, left lying in the grass in the pleasant spot where you ate your lunch. You have heard and read a little about beaching a fish but you have never tried it. You cannot beach the thing here because the bank on which you are standing is two feet above the water. Over there to the left, about twenty yards away, the water meets some mud. Will the mud be firm? Will the hook hold? Can you guide the fish round that clump of reed between you and the mud? Do not panic, but do everything slowly. First, keep a tight line but allow a little more out in the hope that the fish will go further out and give you a chance of steering him out and past those reeds. Walk slowly towards the mud, keep the rod high, thank goodness the fish is still on and he has missed the reeds. Now you are five yards from the mud. There are footprints in it and it looks firm. You are in luck. Tread very carefully and keep about two yards from the water edge. The fish has come up to the surface—a beautiful brown trout. He is tired of being towed around and has turned on his side. Keep the rod vertical and reel in until the leader knot is at the top ring. Now with the greatest care and with firmness draw the fish away from the water, keeping his head just up and out of the mud. Bring him two yards in from the water in one continuous drawing movement. You have made it. A perfect brownie of about two pounds. Small head, deep body and brilliant spots. There is no need to keep shaking, it is all over now and you have beached your first fish. Have a look at the hook, it is right tight in the 'scissors' of the trout's jaw, firmly bedded in the hard bony part. That is why you were lucky, but it does not always work out like this, particularly if you are fishing with small flies and have a lightly-hooked fish.

The chances of beaching a fish successfully are mainly dependent on the strength of the hook hold and the ability to draw the fish from the water in a continuous movement, so that he glides in with the minimum interference from weed, twigs, stones and other similar obstructions. If you pause during the draw-in a powerful fish may find enough strength to flex himself up onto his tail and he will be off like a flash unless he is completely played out.

Getting the bird

It was a dullish afternoon and I was trying a little dry fly casting off Green Lawn at Blagdon. It was not a bad forward cast and I could see the little dark fly sitting up on the ripple about twenty yards out. Swifts were dipping over the water at regular intervals, sweeping down very fast and nipping flies off the surface film. My attention was not really focused on the dry fly in front of me as it should have been, I was peering down into the water to see whether there were any signs of insect life near my waders. Next moment I felt a tremendous take, and was rather surprised to see my line leaving the water in an upward direction. A swift had paid me the compliment of being deceived by my fly, which was now firmly bedded into the fluttering bird. The swift fell into the water and I retrieved the line as carefully as possible with the wretched bird lashing around in the water surface. By some miracle the hook barb was not in the bird's beak or throat: he had obviously changed his mind at the last instant but the hook was firmly bedded in one wing. John was fishing nearby and after a few words of cynical congratulation helped me unhook the fly, by which time the drenched swift was in a very sad state. We found a nearby bush and after some gentle drying with a piece of cloth set the bird to rest. I gave him a few crumbs under the shelter from an old sandwich and he began to perk up. I ignored John's suggestion that perhaps he would like a few sips of water. We resumed fishing and half an hour later saw the swift fly off apparently none the worse for his most unhappy experience.

Meat instead of fish

I was going through one of those really bad spells when nothing would go right. My casting was dreadful and I was near some sheep grazing on the north shore of Weir Wood. Twice I retrieved a hook which had become embedded in an embankment as the result of a drooping back cast, and I sat down for a rest in the hope that I would soon recover such little of the casting skill I had acquired to date. Five minutes or so later I resumed fishing and on the second false cast was taken fiercely from behind, as my pathetically low and falling back cast resulted in the fly taking a firm hook hold in the rump of a sheep. Off went the sheep, taking line fast, and despite my feelings of general despair I was sufficiently conscious to realize that this was not the occasion for trying to keep a tight line. Somehow or other I managed to lay the rod down safely on some grass with the reel pointing up and for the next few minutes I chased the wretched animal, ably assisted by a nearby fisherman who was far too friendly to curse me for my idiotic performance. Between us the hook was released from its woolly bed and the sheep scampered away. Although the chances of your catching a sheep on a fly may be fairly remote, it is worth remembering that sheep frequently graze on the margins of reservoirs, and if you decide to have a doze during a warm afternoon always put your rod up onto some form of a rest to prevent the possibility of its being trampled upon either by sheep or quite accidentally by another fisherman who may be passing by.

Emergency repairs

I was carrying my rod in the orthodox fashion with the reel forward and tip behind. Someone called and I looked round to answer, and in doing so hooked the rod tip over the barb of a barbed wire fence— a slight accidental movement which resulted in the tip ring becoming wrenched out of alignment and loosened as well. I was short of time and was looking forward to the evening's fishing. The rod could not be used like this and I had no form of whipping skill at the time. Very fortunately I had some Elastoplast strips in a tin which I used to take around as part of my gear. By cutting off the lint I made a good enough repair with two strips of the elastic bandage to secure the tip ring firmly for the evening. A coil of waterproof Sellotape takes up very little room in your pocket and might be worth carrying in case of a similar accident to the your tackle, or to that of another fisherman in temporary trouble.

Occasionally after two or three seasons you may find there is some slight slack in the ferrule joint of your rod which results in the two sections twisting, causing the rings to go out of alignment. A blade of grass placed along the side of the male ferrule before sliding home into the female socket will normally make a tight fit. Eventually if this trouble persists you will have to send the rod for an overhaul. A metal ferrule can be given a smear of beeswax to cure any slack as another temporary solution to this problem.

Trouble with leaders and flies

On this occasion you came out without checking your oddments, and the grease tin and detergent pad have been left behind. If you want to ensure your leader will float for delicate nymphing or dry fly work, dry it thoroughly and then draw the nylon to and fro through your hair so that nature's grease or the barber's artificial can provide a coating on the nylon. If you are mainly bald like me then run the nylon across your scalp—there usually seems to be some form of natural grease which adds lustre to a sun-burned pate, enough at any rate to keep thin nylon afloat for a reasonable while. Alternatively you may have a bag in your pocket with the remains of a sandwich left over. There will be enough butter or margarine on the paper to grease a leader for quite a while. A tiny smear of butter from a sandwich pack rubbed into your fingers and then onto a dry fly will keep it afloat for a long while.

If you want a leader to sink, some advocate wiping it with mud. This is not always successful and a better answer lies in really sucking the nylon to get it covered with saliva. Better still, if you have caught a fish earlier draw the leader right through his gill cover, and the slime will make a leader sink like a stone without any difficulty.

All fishermen get tangles in leaders at some time. If you have a really bad tangle and the fish are on the move it is quicker to tie on a spare fresh leader rather than waste valuable time unravelling the mess. If you are without a spare leader (and you ought not to be) then the first thing to do is to take off the fly or flies. Do not pull anything tight and keep the coils as open as possible. If the light is fading hold the tangle up towards the sky where you will get better light. Never leave a tangle with a tight wind knot in a thin section. As mentioned when dealing with the tying of leaders, a tight knot of this type will cut into the main strand and may easily cost you a lost fish. If you get furious with the whole mess of tangled nylon, do not throw it away in disgust. A bird or other creature may become entangled and suffer a great deal as a result of your carelessness. When fishing amongst weed you will find that the blood knots joining the sections of your leader may become clogged with weed, and likewise the fly hook. A careful check to keep the leader and fly free of weed should be made before each cast and retrieve, otherwise you will find that the leader sinks too deeply for the best result, and a weed-clogged fly is useless for deceiving a trout. Always use small hooks when fishing amongst weed—they will offer much less resistance to clogging and knotless, continuous, tapered leaders are a great aid under weedy conditions.

Quite often, when retrieving close to or among weed beds the fly will become hooked in a strand of weed. Never try to free the fly by a brisk twitch with a cane rod because you may quite possibly strain or even break the rod tip. The correct way to free a caught-up fly is to set the rod tip pointing towards the obstruction and give a gentle pull on the fly line so that the line and leader take the strain without any harm to the rod tip. Always check a fly after it has become stuck in weed or other obstruction because the hook bend or barb may have become damaged when it was pulled free. When fishing among weed always check that the fly or flies are free before making a back cast. If a fly is lodged in weed and you go for a sharp back cast you might easily damage the rod tip. Hollow glass rods can withstand tougher treatment than cane rods but both types deserve careful handling to prevent overstraining the top section, and more care is required when fishing amongst weed than under deeper clear water conditions.

The late take

Fish have been moving and there has been a good evening rise. You tried Sedge tactics, then the Buzzer, but the fish were very difficult and would not take your patterns no matter how carefully they were presented and retrieved. Now it is nearly dark. The rise has died down and you have decided to give it another quarter of an hour before packing up. Perhaps there will be a few big fish moving into the shallows. Tie on a lure, make sure of the knot and wipe the leader with your pad of detergent to ensure quick sinking. Hold the lure between your fingers and dip it into the water, then squeeze it. This will get air out of the dressing and make the lure sink quickly. No need for a long cast, perhaps ten or fifteen yards at most. You see the floating line straighten in what remains of the red sun glow on the water. A pause to enable the lure to sink and then a very gradual retrieve to avoid line wake and surface disturbance. Towards the end of the retrieve and just before the haul for a back cast you think you see a very slight deflection in the floating line. Probably a piece of weed, or was it a fish? Two neat false casts and again out goes the line, leader and lure. A further pause and very slow retrieve. No, it seems that everything has gone very dead and the air has chilled, probably putting the trout down for the rest of the night. You might as well try one more cast before packing up. You are about to make a back cast and just as your rod comes up to about the eleven o'clock point you are taken savagely by a trout right at the surface as the lure is on the point of lift-off. For about three seconds the fish seems almost on—you feel him but have no chance of tightening because with your casting arm at the maximum upright position you cannot strike into the fish which followed that lure for a long time and finally decided to take it just as it was on the point of escaping from the water surface. There are endless ways of losing a good fish and I seem to fall for this one time and time again. The main thing to remember is that as long as you have a fly in the water and are making a deliberate and careful retrieve there is always the possibility that a trout may be following it right up to the moment of lift-off for a back cast. The moral lies in keeping a careful watch on the line just at the moment before the leader is about to leave the water, and if you have the slightest suspicion that a trout is following the fly pause a second or two to give time for a take which can be controlled rather than risk a savage snatch which will usually result in a broken point, lost fly and injured fish.

Here then we have looked at some of the various accidents which can happen during our bank fishing. Some can be serious, other disheartening or plain ridiculous, whichever way you choose to judge them. As I said at the outset, they have all happened to me, but fortunately I have been spared any permanent injury despite mistaken wading. If you are blessed with a sense of humour, can laugh at your own mistakes and sympathize with those made by others you must end up by acquiring a little more know-how which will add to your general knowledge and experience of bank fishing for reservoir trout.

1. Sweeney Todd

2. Sedge Pupa

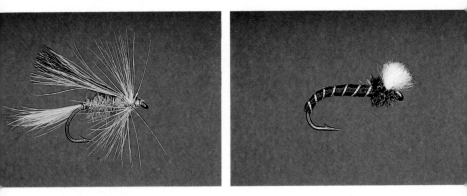

3. Hatching Sedge

4. Buzzer

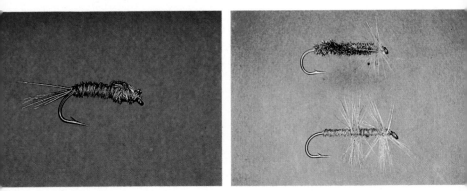

5. Pheasant Tail Nymph

6. Stickfly & Double
Hackled Stickfly

Photograph 42. Six patterns for a season. These patterns are recommended for use under various tactical situations which arise during the course of a season's bank fishing. Chapter 10 describes modifications which can be made in the dressings of these flies as well as ways of fishing them.

10

Six Patterns for a Season

I have previously stressed the importance of size, depth and presentation when considering the use of a particular fly for each tactical situation, and have recommended that the beginner should keep to a few flies and learn how to fish them correctly so that he acquires the feeling of confidence which is essential to success. For this reason I am going to suggest six well tried fly patterns, but we will consider the merits of having these six patterns in different sizes with modifications in body colouring where appropriate. We must also have regard to the depth at which our six patterns are to be fished. If we are going to fish deep, then our fly must be weighted with fine copper wire or lead foil under the dressing so it sinks rapidly to the depth we have selected as right for the circumstances. On the other hand, we may need our fly to work just beneath the surface film—or possibly to sit right up on the ripple as a floating dry fly.

If you fish these six patterns at the appropriate times during the course of a season I am sure you will receive many offers to your fly—but it will be up to you to tighten or strike into your fish at the moment you think fit—and this timing of the strike is something you will learn as your general experience widens.

The six patterns illustrated in photograph 42 facing page 147 have been tied for me by Les Sawyer, the Bailiff at Bough Beech. It was he who gave me my first lessons in fly tying several winters ago, and whilst I now tie most of the limited numbers of patterns I use during the course of a season they do not have the professional finish which is so pleasing for the purpose of illustration. The flies I tie are good enough to deceive fish but they are by no means perfect examples of the fly dresser's art.

I am very particular about the quality of hooks and have found those by Mustad of Norway and Yorkshire Stronghold by Mackenzie Philps to be very reliable. Some shop bought flies are somewhat loosely tied to inferior hooks and I most strongly recommend you to learn the basic elements of fly tying because not only will you save a great deal of expense but you will gain tremendous satisfaction from catching a trout on a fly of your own tying. There are excellent books on the subject and several are referred to in Appendix B.

I believe a beginner should concentrate on learning to fish a few flies correctly—because in this way he will avoid wasting precious fishing time by unnecessary changes when fish are on the feed.

I have mentioned the need for weighting certain of the tyings beneath the dressing and you may wonder how you will be able to distinguish a weighted from a non-weighted fly of the same pattern. An easy solution lies in painting a small blob of red nail varnish on the whipped finish of weighted patterns—and it helps to keep them in a separate tin from those which are not colour coded in this way.

Here then are six patterns for you to concentrate upon and suggested methods of fishing them in the course of a season's bank fishing.

(1) *Sweeney Todd* (Photograph 42[1])
This fly is one of many designed by that great angler Richard Walker who has contributed so much to every aspect of fishing.

Dressing
Hook: Sizes 12 to 6, long shank.
Tying silk: Black.
Body: Black floss ribbed with fine silver thread. Just behind the wing root make two or three turns of D.F. magenta wool.
Throat hackle: Crimson cock hackle fibres.
Wing: Squirrel tail hairs dyed black.

Tactics
(a) In the early part of the season fish the largest size as a lure with sinking line. Some weighting beneath the dressing will assist sinking. Trout will follow this lure for a long time, so be patient

when searching the hidden depths and fish out your cast systematically with variations in the speed of retrieve from fast to very slow. Cover a different section of water with each cast and preferably cast across the wind.

(b) As the season warms up tie this fly to a 12′ 0″ leader and fish it fast beneath the surface with a floating line. Watch the junction between line tip and leader and tighten at the slightest suspicion of a take. Work the fly at different depths and at different speeds but keep to the floating line.

(c) In warm dull conditions when fish are feeding in the upper levels tie on a size 10 or 12 Sweeney Todd—keep to your floating line and cover the rises with as delicate a cast as you can make. If there is good ripple on the surface fish the fly fast; in calm conditions use the same size fly but a weighted pattern and fish it as previously recommended for leaded nymph tactics. In calm water the leader must be treated with sinking compound so that it sinks beneath the surface film and avoids scaring a deep lying trout by line shadow.

(d) If you have assessed fish to be feeding on midge pupae and your buzzer patterns have been either rejected or disregarded, tie on a size 10 or 12 Sweeney Todd and fish it as for buzzer tactics, keeping the fly high in the surface film. The smaller version of this pattern is a very useful alternative to the buzzer patterns when fish are being difficult.

(e) After the surface activity of a good evening rise has died down tie on the size 8 Sweeney Todd and fish it very patiently through the area of past feeding. If the water is calm, fish the lure slowly but if there is still some ripple speed up the retrieve. As previously mentioned, large trout frequently cruise into the margins at dusk and as long as you fish this lure systematically through varying arcs it is quite possible you may have a very positive take from a good fish just before it is time to pack up. In this situation be prepared for a sudden take just as you are lifting off for a back cast because trout will follow this lure right up to the last moment.

(f) When you have seen large trout beating up the shallow margins in their wild forage for sticklebacks, minnow or fry you must bring the Sweeney Todd into action without delay. Firstly, keep well back from the water's edge and watch the general line of attack by the trout. Try and get some background cover, or better still, get down on one knee. Tie on a size 8 Sweeney Todd and cast it with floating line about 1 yard ahead of the bow-wave which a large trout creates when he is on this type of activity. As soon as the fly hits the water begin a fast and continuous retrieve so that the fly skates just beneath the surface amongst the scattering small fry. It is quite possible the trout will make a mistake and you will need a stout point to your leader for these tactics because if the trout does take your lure it is likely to be a savage affair and you must rely on a good hook and strong nylon for the end result.

(2) *Sedge Pupa* (Photograph 42[2])

This is one of the many patterns developed by those great fishermen John Goddard and Cliff Henry. The pattern represents the pupae of various sedge flies during their ascension to the surface film in the early stage of transformation to the winged adult. Sedge flies are of great importance to the trout and therefore to the fishermen and from the first time you see sedge flies fluttering around the margins the Sedge Pupae patterns must be brought into action. The artificials are dressed in various colours to match the most common colours of the naturals but the tyings are all the same.

Dressing
Hook: Sizes 12 to 8, long shank.
Tying silk: Brown.
Body: Seal's fur, either cream, brown, olive green or orange.
Ribbing: Oval silver.
Thorax: Dark brown condor herl (or cock pheasant tail fibres).
Wing case: Light brown condor herl (or hen pheasant tail fibres).
Hackle: Two turns natural cock hackle.

Tactics
(a) For the early part of the season I find it pays to have several patterns weighted with fine copper wire beneath the body dressing because trout will sometimes take this fly at a greater depth. At this depth the Sedge Pupa will be taking shape after its emergence from the earlier larval stage.

(b) The Sedge Pupa is generally best fished with floating line and about 12' 0" leader and the fly should be cast into the area of sedge activity and retrieved fairly quickly just beneath the surface film. The choice of colour can best be judged by catching a natural sedge fly as it flutters past and matching the body colour of your artificial to that of the natural.

In calm water the Sedge Pupa must be retrieved gently to avoid line wake but on rippled water the retrieve can be quite fast so that the fly rides high beneath the surface. In all cases the leader should be treated with sinking compound so that it cuts beneath the surface film.

(c) When retrieving the Sedge Pupa pause at intervals so the fly has time to sink a little and then continue the retrieve on the sink and draw principle so that the fly moves at slightly varying depths. In dull light use the larger sized hook and in brighter light the smaller sizes. As always you must give full concentration to the point at which the fly line joins the leader and if there is the slightest dip, slowing down or other signal you must tighten in response to the trout's offer to your fly.

(3) *Hatching Sedge* (Photograph 42[3])

This pattern is as devised by Cliff Henry, a reservoir fisherman of outstanding ability, who, for the greater part of his fishing tactics, uses imitations of the natural insects which are available to the trout throughout the season. He has very many years of experience and conducts the most painstaking research into all forms of insect life, and matches his artificial flies to deceive the trout with consistent success. It was he who taught us to fish the Hatching Sedge during periods of prolific hatches of sedge flies, at which time the trout are preoccupied with taking the naturals at their point of emergence as adults after shedding their pupal cases.

Dressing
Hook: Size 10 or 12, down eye.
Tying silk: Olive green.
Tail: Golden pheasant crest.
Body: Green seal's fur.
Ribbing: Fine gold thread.
Wing: Natural grey squirrel tail. (With white tips clipped off.)
Hackle: Ginger cock.

When this fly is required as a dry fly the hackle turns are increased to give added buoyancy.

Variations in body material can be made so that the colour of the artificial may match the colour of the hatching naturals—and again for the purpose of comparison it pays to catch a newly hatched sedge fly as it flutters around the margin and tie on an artificial with similar body colour.

Tactics

The beauty of this fly is that it can either be fished as a wet fly just beneath the surface film, or with the application of floatant it will sit up as a dry fly when dry fly tactics are called for. This fly is fished with floating line and the leader must be about 12' 0" long treated with sinking compound. When sedge flies are hatching there is usually a slashing rise by the trout and it is at this period the Hatching Sedge should be cast into the rise rings and retrieved fairly quickly, because it pays to cover as large an area as possible when trout are moving fast and feeding upon the adult sedge flies.

Some fishermen prefer to use the Hatching Sedge tied as a dropper with a Sedge Pupa on the point and this can be a very successful combination for sedge tactics. The dropper link needs to be short and stout so that the dropper fly does not become twisted around the main length of leader. In well rippled water the retrieve can be very fast because in this way the flies will be fishing the surface film and it is at this level the Hatching Sedge is most effective. As a general rule I am not very keen on the use of droppers in fading light as there can be a waste of valuable fishing time if a bad tangle occurs. My own preference is to fish the Hatching Sedge as a single point fly and if fished wet the retrieve can be varied from very fast in rippled water to a mild tweak in conditions of flat calm. Remember to try this pattern as a dry fly when there is sedge activity around the weed beds. Cast it out and leave it to 'wander' on the edge of the ripple and you may have a very positive rise to your fly.

(4) *Buzzer* (Photograph 42[4])

It is impossible to overstress the importance of midge pupae as a major part of the feed of reservoir trout and you will remember that fishermen have adopted the name Buzzer to cover the variety of midge pupae which abound in the majority of reservoirs.

For this pattern we must have tyings in different colours because it is proven that trout can be most selective in their preference for one colour at a particular time. All tyings are the same but in addition to variations in colour it is well worth while having a few weighted patterns also—because these can be used effectively to represent the midge pupae at greater depth as opposed to the pupae in the surface film.

Dressing

Hook: Sizes 14 to 10, wide gape, down eye.

Body: Either black, red, orange, green or brown in colour and of floss, shredded wool or dubbed seal's fur. The tying silk to match the body colour.

Ribbing: Oval silver.

Head: Bronze peacock herl.

Breathing filaments: White D.F. wool.

Some fly dressers imitate the tiny caudal fins at the tail and these may be added by using several points of white cock hackle fibres. The butts of the same fibres may be used as the breathing filaments in place of the white wool in the above dressing.

The body colours vary to imitate those of the natural pupae and are usually black, red, green, orange/silver or black with a red collar. Body materials can be of floss silk but other tyings with shredded wool or dubbed seal's fur are often successful. The latter materials seem to give a more succulent appearance to the fly.

Tactics

(a) For early season tactics weighted buzzer patterns are required and as previously explained this weighting is achieved by providing a copper wire underlay to the body dressing. Make up a leader about 12' 0" long with a stout short dropper link about 4' back from the point. Tie on a weighted red buzzer at the point and a weighted black buzzer on the dropper. Treat the leader with sinking compound and attach it to your floating line. I suggest the red buzzer at the deeper level because this will represent the red larva or bloodworm which you will recall is the earliest stage of buzzer life. Cast over spots which are likely holding grounds in deeper water of undisturbed margins and make a methodical series of retrieves covering a wide arc of water. Once the leader has touched down count up to about twenty before beginning a very slow retrieve— giving an occasional little jerk to the line which in turn will give animation to the flies. A take will be registered by deflection of the joint between floating line-tip and leader and you must concentrate on that point during the whole of each retrieve. Your rod tip must be touching the water surface so that an immediate strike may be transmitted to the fish.

(b) Some fishermen prefer to use weighted buzzers in combination with a sinking line and this is good practice where there is very deep water to be searched. The use of sinking line requires an adjustment in the method of retrieve so that offers to your flies may be registered. With a sinking line the joint between line tip and leader is completely submerged and in order to register offers by the trout the rod tip must be kept right down to the water surface and a little coil of slack line is left visible between rod tip and water level. If the coil moves tighten immediately because that is your signal that the flies have been mouthed or accepted.

(c) When you have assessed trout to be feeding on midge pupae suspended in the surface film very delicate tactics are required. I use a floating line with about 4' 0" of heavy nylon (about 30 lb B.S.) knotted to the whipped loop of the line tip. To this heavy link of nylon I blood-knot a 12' 0" continuous tapered leader with a point of about 4 lb B.S. and tie on one selected buzzer to the point. The leader and link are treated with sinking compound for its full length except the last 3" next to the fly and this 3" section is greased. The effect of this treatment will be to have a submerged leader except for the little section near the fly which will ride just under the surface film. I find the black buzzer to be reliable in dull or fading light but under brighter conditions you must try to match the colour of your fly to that of the naturals. The Footballer is a very good all round standby fly for buzzer tactics and do not forget the value of the small Sweeney Todd for the same purpose.

When fishing your imitation in the surface film under calm conditions it is essential to avoid line wake. Buzzer hatches frequently occur in calm water—in the early morning—during the warmer parts of the day and again in the evening. These hatches will often occur in 'calm lanes' just where the ripple meets calm water and for this type of fishing a very careful and delicate retrieve is required with your full concentration upon the joint between line tip and leader. If you see a bulge or rise near your fly tighten at once because the fish may have mouthed the fly without your feeling anything.

In fading light towards the end of an evening rise you will find the take to a buzzer is usually quite positive—but in brighter light it is a very different matter. Smaller patterns should be fished in bright light and larger ones in the evening or in dull light.

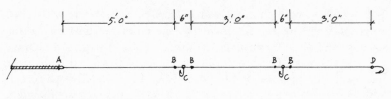

A   8 lb B.S. leader joined to whipped loop
     at tip of fly line.
B   Blood knots.
C   Straight eye hooks.
D   Down eye hook.   Figure 20. A leader for Buzzer tactics.

(d) As an alternative to fishing a single buzzer there is a very good method which Cliff Henry was good enough to explain to me in detail. For this method the buzzer patterns are tied direct to a continuous leader of about 8 lb B.S. throughout its entire length— generally as indicated in figure 20. You will see in this case we have three buzzers tied direct to the leader. The intermediate flies are tied with straight-eye hooks and the point fly has a down-eye hook. By the use of straight-eye hooks the intermediate buzzers can 'travel' between the blood knots. In order to keep the buzzers high in the surface film the entire leader can be greased if you are fishing well rippled water—but in calmer conditions it is better to treat the leader with sinking compound and smear a little grease to each of the flies. In calm water the retrieve of this type of leader must be very delicate and slow—but in well rippled water the retrieve can be quite fast—and this fast retrieve will have the effect of keeping the buzzers high up in the surface film amongst the hatching naturals.

When using this continuous leader or the alternative with dropper links, it is as well to put on three different coloured buzzers—because as previously mentioned the trout can be very selective when on this type of feed. It is a good idea to have perhaps three leaders made up on these lines so you may change a leader completely and offer the fish a complete change of body colours. When retrieving a team of three (or more) buzzers you must tighten at the slightest hint of an offer and if you see the flash of a trout as he turns near your leader tighten immediately because he may well have selected and mouthed one of your flies.

It seems that a combination of black, red and green will often lead to success but you must ring the changes and have another leader tied up with an orange/silver buzzer, a black one with a red collar and perhaps the Footballer at the point. Two of my fishing friends and I often tie on a very simply tied buzzer pattern which we call the Convict. The body is of white floss silk ribbed with black button thread up to a simple peacock herl thorax. This pattern is well worth trying amongst the others I have recommended. Fortunately all the buzzer patterns are easy to tie and they are most valuable flies for all forms of reservoir fishing.

Finally, if you catch a fish on buzzer tactics always spoon him immediately and examine the stomach contents. If you find several midge pupae alive and kicking these are the ones the trout has last taken and you must match your artificials to the size and colour of the naturals.

(5) *Pheasant Tail Nymph* (Photograph 42[5])

This is one of similar patterns devised by the great Frank Sawyer and you will remember the quotation on page 93 in which he kindly advised me on the correct method of fishing his weighted nymph patterns. The Pheasant Tail nymph is an excellent pattern for leaded nymph tactics and we must consider opportunities for its use when the right circumstances arise.

Dressing
Hook: Sizes 8 to 14 down eye.
Tying material: Fine copper wire instead of waxed silk.
Tail, body and thorax: Cock pheasant tail fibres.
Method of Tying: The hook is bound with fine copper wire starting from behind the eye and stopping short at the hook bend. Three or four fibres of cock pheasant tail are tied in leaving the tips projecting about ¼" beyond the hook. Wind the copper wire back towards the eye and build up a bold thorax of copper wire. Now wind the pheasant tail fibres towards the eye of the hook covering the copper wire as you go. Tie down the body fibres behind the thorax and then double the fibres back and forward over the thorax to form the wing case. Tie in the butt ends, clip off, and finish the tying with two or three half hitches. Varnish over the copper wire finish.

For added durability the first binding of copper wire may be given a coat of varnish and the feather fibres can be wound while the varnish is wet.

Tactics

Leaded nymph fishing demands delicate and accurate casting using a well tapered leader at least 15′ 0″ long attached to a floating line. I prefer using a continuous tapered leader with a stout butt extension as described in part (c) of Buzzer tactics. For this type of fishing we must search for little bays and marginal weed beds, the corners of dams and those parts of shore line which shelve away steeply to give deep water within easy casting range. Above all we must keep well away from other fishermen in the hope we shall be fishing quiet water which has not been recently disturbed.

The Pheasant Tail nymph is fished as a single point fly and your leader must be thoroughly stretched and treated with sinking compound so that it extends without coiling and sinks immediately beneath the surface film. Methods of fishing may be considered as follows :—

(a) If you spot fish rising in calm water it is quite probable there will be others feeding in the same location at a lower depth and these deep lying feeding fish will not create a rise ring. In these conditions you must be cautious in your approach and stand or kneel well back from the water's edge. Put on a pair of polaroid glasses and spend a few minutes scanning the water. If you see the silver flash caused by a trout as he turns in the deeper water it is quite quite probable he is busy in the weed beds searching out food which is available at that level. The Pheasant Tail nymph is not tied to represent any particular natural insect but its general shape and silhouette are similar to one of the largest groups of aquatic insects —and above all this fly is designed to sink immediately it breaks the water surface.

Once you have decided you are within casting range of deep feeding fish make your first cast parallel to the margin—no more than a yard from the water's edge. If we call this first cast 'nine o'clock' then subsequent casts need to be fanned out to cover a semi-circle between nine and three o'clock. In this way each cast will be to a different piece of water and there will be less disturbance to fish who may be feeding within the semi-circle you have selected for this style of fishing. Your cast must be delicate and from the moment your leaded nymph touches the water surface you must have your eyes pinned on the leader because a deep lying trout will often accept the nymph *as it descends towards him* and the only indication you have is some unnatural quickening as the leader descends through the surface film. You must keep your rod tip right down to the water surface and tighten if you have the slightest suspicion of a take.

(b) Trout will take the Pheasant Tail nymph during a very careful retrieve and you must concentrate upon the joint between line tip and leader and watch for the slightest sign of movement which will occur when the fish mouths or accepts your fly. When retrieving in calm water it is essential to avoid line wake and leaded nymph fishing calls for the very best you can achieve in delicate casting and concentration for signs of a take. Polaroid glasses are a great asset for this type of fishing because they help you to see the deeper lying fish.

(c) The Pheasant Tail nymph is tied in different sizes—the larger ones are for very deep water tactics and the small ones are for careful work in the shallows. The small Pheasant Tail nymph will often be taken by the trout when they are feeding on corixae and the larger patterns are very good for fishing the deeper water when snail are available for the trout. For very deep water tactics you will need to increase the length of your leader to the maximum you can handle.

In shallow water you may see a trout showing his tail and this will indicate he is grubbing about the bottom searching out feed at that level, and whenever you spot the tail of a feeding fish you must turn to leaded nymph tactics without delay. A number of fishermen regard flat calm as a hopeless condition for trout fishing and although it is not easy it is always worth while turning to leaded nymph tactics under these conditions. During the drought and brilliant sunlight of 1976 water temperatures rose to exceptional heights and although there were times when there were no signs of a rise, with the aid of polaroids it was possible to see the flash caused by a trout turning in relatively shallow water. By the application of careful leaded nymph tactics the occasional trout would be caught under the most difficult conditions of flat calm and bright light. Without doubt the Pheasant Tail nymph is a very fine fly—but it is designed to be fished in the manner recommended by Frank Sawyer and this calls for a great deal of patience and intense concentration.

(d) The Pheasant Tail nymph can be put to great use where fish are feeding amongst the marginal weed beds with deeper layers of water available as lies for the trout. A methodical search with this nymph will often produce good results even though there may be no signs of surface feeding fish. Alternatively if you have spotted fish feeding with a deliberate head and tail rise form you must try to place your nymph inside the rise ring and in this type of fishing it is very probable the take will occur while the weighted nymph is sinking and for this reason you must tighten if there is the slightest unusual movement in the length of leader which has not yet disappeared beneath the surface film.

(e) You will remember my earlier reference to 'float' fishing—whereby a large bushy dry fly is tied to a dropper link several feet back from the point of the leader—and a small leaded nymph is tied at the point. A small Pheasant Tail nymph is ideal for this arrangement and whilst these tactics will upset a purist they can be put to very good use if there is well rippled water beyond marginal weed beds. The leader is neatly cast so that the large dry fly bobs up and down in the ripple, and this movement will cause lifelike movement in the small Pheasant Tail nymph suspended several feet beneath the surface. This movement in the deeper nymph may induce a deep lying trout to accept the fly and there will be a positive signal at which you must tighten as the dry fly dips in answer to the trout's acceptance of the nymph.

Whichever tactical approach you choose to adopt for fishing the Pheasant Tail nymph there is one very important matter to check whenever you are fishing this or other weighted patterns of flies—namely checking the leader for wind knots. The additional weight of these flies—whether big or small—tends to create wind knots, and no matter how good your casting may be, it will pay to make a regular check to see that a wind knot has not developed in your leader when fishing any weighted fly. You will remember that a single wind knot can weaken the breaking strain of nylon to a dangerous extent, and the chances of getting wind knots are very real—particularly when fishing a heavily weighted nymph on a fine point—so keep checking.

(6) *Stickfly* (Photograph 42[6])

The true Stickfly is as dressed in the upper part of photograph No. 42(6) and an adaptation of the original appears in the lower part. You will see that the difference between the original and adaptation is the additional set of hackles set about central in the long body.

Dressing

Hook: Size 8 or 10, long shank.

Tying silk: Brown.

Body: Peacock herl or fibres from cock pheasant tail.

Ribbing: Brown silk or fine copper wire.

Hackle: Natural red game cock.

For durability the hook shank can be coated with varnish and the body material is dressed over while the varnish is still tacky.

For the adaptation an additional set of fine cock hackle is dressed sparsely to give the appearance in the lower part of photograph 42 (6).

I do not think this fly was ever tied as an exact imitation of a real creature but it is a remarkably good fly in both the original and adapted versions. I have purposely included this pattern for the beginner's attention because without doubt trout find both the original and adapted versions of great interest and the tactics for using this valuable fly must be considered in detail.

(a) At the start of the season when trout are lying in deeper waters the single hackled Stickfly must be tried in combination with a sunk line. For this purpose an underlay of fine copper wire is used beneath the fine slim body dressing so that the fly sinks readily into deeper water. It is probable the silhouette of this pattern resembles a number of deep living creatures and the fly must be worked slowly into likely holding grounds which will interest the deep lying trout. We must explore the corners of dams, sections of the bank where deeper water is found within easy casting range, and we must fan our casts so that a methodical search is made in the deeper water. The retrieve must be very slow—perhaps an inch or two at a time when the weighted fly is thought to be just above the bottom of the marginal levels. This fly may have the appearance of various larvae, caddis or other slow moving deep water creatures during the early part of their life cycle and for this reason we must be patient in our exploration of the deeper waters when using this pattern. Perhaps an occasional jerk to the retrieve will give a little animation to the fly—and again the 'sink and draw' method of retrieve must be brought into action so that further lifelike movement is imparted to the fly.

With this weighted Stickfly we shall be fishing in deep water before fish start rising to feed in the upper levels—and whilst for the most part the use of the weighted pattern will be confined to perhaps April and early May, there is no reason why it should not be used again in August and September when fish may be proving difficult to interest at the surface, but willing to accept the fly at greater depth.

(b) As an alternative to the weighted Stickfly used with sunken line, we must experiment with the floating line coupled with a long and well tapered leader treated with sinking mixture and a single weighted pattern of the original single hackled Stickfly tied to the point. With this tackle we shall cast into the vicinity of rising fish and the method of retrieve and general tactics explained for leaded nymph fishing will be appropriate. Your signs of a take will be in deflection, slowing down, straightening, or unusual movement at the joint between line tip and leader—and as always with leaded nymph fishing you must fan your casts to cover as wide an arc of water as you are able, starting with your first cast close to the margin, and altering the angle until dead ahead and thence back through the 180° to the opposite margin. In this way a methodical exploration of different sections of water is achieved without undue disturbance to fish who may be feeding in the locality you have selected as being suitable for the leaded nymph approach.

(c) The adapted version of the Stickfly has the additional central sparse hackle and is very similar to a slim-line version of the Wormfly minus the red tags of the latter. This fly is sometimes used as a weighted pattern—for which tactics (a) and (b) are appropriate, but for the most exciting results it should be used as an unweighted single point fly fished very fast across wind and high in the surface film. When trout are rising to surface feed it is quite remarkable how they will follow a fast retrieved double hackled Stickfly, leaving the take until the very last moment—quite often at that instant when you are least able to strike effectively, i.e. when preparing for a sharp back cast. For this reason if you see a high swimming trout following your fastly retrieved Stickfly you must give a deliberate pause at the end of the retrieve so that the trout has the opportunity of a positive take before the fly is whipped off the surface film under his nose.

In rough water this fly can be stripped back across the surface as fast as you can possibly manage and even though fish may not be showing it is not unusual for this fast moving imitation to provoke either fury, or greed, to any fish who may see it and the take during these very fast surface retrieves is a very positive affair. For this reason, when fishing the double hackled Stickfly fast across the surface the leader point needs to be somewhat stouter than would otherwise be required. The leader itself should be liberally treated with sinking mixture for these fast retrieve tactics.

When using fast retrieve tactics for the double hackled Stickfly we must cast to the best of our ability amongst surface feeding fish— and just as soon as the fly touches the surface start to strip back line as fast as possible so that the fly literally skates across the water surface to induce interest in the trout. Keep the rod tip close to the water and mind you do not tread on the retrieved line as it falls at your feet. Above all, work the fly high in the water with the greatest speed you can impart. Be prepared for smash takes and always pause at the end of each retrieve to give the trout an opportunity of accepting the fly before it disappears with your back cast. Fan your casts to cover as wide an arc as wind conditions will permit and once you have interested one fish in your fast moving fly keep at it until you induce a definite take. At times trout seem to go mad after this pattern—quite often during periods of intense sedge activity —but there are no hard and fast conditions which dictate the use of this fly. Always try this pattern in good ripple to surface feeding fish no matter whether you have assessed the rises to be to Sedge, Buzzer or any other hatch. It is a great standby and the fast moving tactics must be explored to the maximum when trout are really moving and feeding in the upper levels regardless of light conditions, be they bright, dull or nearly dark.

(d) As a complete opposite to the tactics described for the very fast retrieve, the double hackled pattern has yet another role to play in totally different conditions—namely in calmer water during the day time—and again during the last five minutes before packing up time at the end of a good evening rise.

The Stickfly in calm water can be used as a very effective dry fly— all that is needed is a slight application of Permaflote or Mucilin— but make sure that the floatant is applied to both sets of hackle tips. If you treat the fly thus and stand him in a saucer of water you will see he sits up beautifully in a well balanced manner with the hackle tips just penetrating the surface film. Here then we have a most versatile fly. When used dry, the Stickfly must be cast into the calmer water where fish are known to lie—preferably just off the marginal weed beds and the fly is best left stationary. The leader must be treated with sinking compound so that it is submerged beneath the surface film. If a light ripple occurs then the rippled water will give animation to the fly sitting in the surface film, but if there is no ripple then a delicate tweak to the fly line will cause the fly to move two or three inches. It is quite probable a patient spell of fishing along these lines will pay off, because a deep lying fish may well decide to rise and take this pattern with a resounding whorl. Remember these tactics when crane flies are being blown from the bank onto the marginal waters. You may not have an exact imitation but the double hackled Stickfly fished dry is often taken when fish are preoccupied with this type of feed.

In rougher water the double hackled Stickfly will often prove successful fished as a dry fly and left to 'wander' amongst the wavelets. Keep your rod tip low, mend the belly out of the leader, and tighten as soon as you see the fish turn—he has probably accepted the fly before you feel him.

Some fishermen use the double hackled Stickfly as a point fly with a Hatching Sedge pattern on the dropper. This can be a deadly combination in skilled hands but I am not very fond of droppers in fading light as I am prone towards tangles under these conditions, and for this reason I prefer to use the Stickfly as a single point fly fished in the variety of ways we have looked at.

(e) The last tactical approach to the great versatility of the double hackled Stickfly can often be put to good effect during the final minutes of a summer evening's fishing after a good rise has died down. Treat the leader with sinking compound and remove any traces of floatant fom the fly with detergent. Cast out quietly in the vicinity of marginal weed beds and allow a few seconds for the fly to sink to perhaps one foot or so beneath the surface. Lower your rod tip to within 3″ of the water and begin a very slow retrieve. You cannot see the junction of floating line and leader because it is too dark so leave a little coil of line beneath your rod tip and the water surface. As soon as you have the impression that your line is 'moving away from you', tighten as this could be the best fish of the day. It is at this late hour big fish patrol the margins and the Stickfly will give a good hook hold for playing a large fish under rather difficult conditions near weed in fading light.

Here then we have explored some seasonal tactics which may be tried by the beginner—involving the use of no more than six well tried basic patterns—but with variations in colour, size, weighting and minor modifications to dressings as described. It is quite beyond the scope of this book to describe the elements of fly dressing but some excellent books for beginners and more experienced fishermen are referred to in Appendix B. If you persevere with a limited number of patterns you will gain confidence and avoid wasting valuable fishing time with needless changes. Remember that size, depth and method of presentation are the three most important matters to keep in mind when bank fishing. Many fishermen enjoy great success using no more than two or three different patterns throughout an entire season, whilst others who prefer to offer the fish imitations of natural creatures may use a great number of very carefully tied flies to match the natural insects which are available at different stages in the season. The choice is entirely a matter for individual preference and as long as your objective is enjoyable fishing with reasonable success you will gradually develop your own style and succeed when bank fishing for reservoir trout.

Appendix A

How to get information about reservoir fishing facilities

First, as you make new friends during your reservoir fishing you are sure to get first hand advice about other opportunities within reasonable distance of home and probably some valuable information about places to stay if you decide to go away for a fishing holiday. Apart from receiving information from your fishing friends the following notes may help you to obtain further details.

Where to Fish: This is *The Field* guide to fishing at sea or in rivers, lakes and reservoirs throughout the world but with specially detailed and well-indexed information on facilities in the British Isles. The '78/'79 edition recently published by Harmsworth Press Ltd includes an excellent map and provides clearly presented details of where and what types of game, coarse or sea fishing are available. It is exceptionally well indexed, easy to follow and includes a lot of interesting detail about notable fish caught in different waters in past years, and the location of River Boards and Authorities responsible for management of numerous fisheries.

Still Water Fly Fishing by T. C. Ivens published in 1970 by André Deutsch: Once again I must refer to this most comprehensive book. Chapter nineteen titled 'Where to fish for trout in reservoirs' includes a directory of reservoirs throughout England and Wales with further advice as to where correspondence should be addressed for further information in each case.

The Editors of the monthly magazines *Angling* and *Trout & Salmon* have kindly informed me they will be pleased to provide any information on reservoir fishing facilities throughout the British Isles and this arrangement will be particularly helpful to a beginner, who should write for such information as he needs. *Angling* includes a monthly report on all branches of the sport but there are usually some very interesting articles on reservoir fishing and in

Trout & Salmon you will find regular reviews on fly fishing tackle design as well as numerous interesting articles on every aspect of reservoir fishing.

Appendix B

Books recommended for reference and further study

GENERAL KNOWLEDGE

Still Water Fly Fishing by T. C. Ivens: The revised and enlarged third edition published by André Deutsch in 1970 is a modern guide to all methods of fishing for trout in reservoirs and lakes. The author writes with great enthusiasm and a beginner should read and read again his advice on the essential elements of learning to present a limited selection of fly patterns in order to deceive a reservoir trout.

Trout Flies of Still Water by John Goddard, published in 1969 by A. & C. Black: The subject of this book is The Natural Fly, its Matching Artificial and Fishing Technique. This book includes over 130 coloured photographs of superb quality and the results of the author's painstaking research and fly fishing skill are put on record for all time. A truly magnificent book for more detailed study after the beginner becomes interested in knowing more of the life history of the numerous creatures devoured by reservoir trout, and for learning ways of deceiving the fish by a suitable fly.

Fly Fishing Tactics on Still Water by Geoffrey Bucknall, published by Muller: In this book the author guides the newcomer to reservoir fishing through a system of fly selection and seasonal tactics which will lead to success. Some of the author's fly dressings are described in detail and the book as a whole is most instructive for the beginner in reservoir fishing and for others of more experience.

A Fly Fisher's Life by Charles Ritz, published by Reinhardt: The latest edition of this classic was published in 1972. Although primarily for the river fisherman it is a wonderfully illustrated book and I recommend our beginner to obtain a copy on loan from the library and to study the excellent diagrams and photographs of fly line casting; also to memorize the author's repeated advice on the importance of keeping a high back cast, coupled with line hand haul to ensure an accurate and delicate forward cast. In reservoir fishing a great deal of casting is required and you will find it a lot easier to achieve if you follow the advice given in this fine book.

Teach Yourself Fly Fishing by Maurice Wiggin, published by Teach Yourself Books Ltd: This light-hearted book covers fly fishing on rivers, lakes and reservoirs. The illustrations and line drawings are first class and the beginner will find this book very easy to read. The drawings of natural flies and matching artificials are particularly good.

FLY TYING

Fly Tying Problems and their Answers by John Veniard and Donald Downs, published by A. & C. Black; *Fly Dressers Guide, Further Guide to Fly Dressing, Reservoir and Lake Flies,* all by John Veniard and published by A. & C. Black: Each of these fine books is regarded as being of top class in this fascinating and specialized art.

Fly Tying for Beginners by Geoffrey Bucknall, published by Angling Times. This is a first class, well illustrated book.

Fly Dressing Innovations by Richard Walker, published by Ernest Benn Ltd. Richard Walker is a regular contributor to *Trout & Salmon* and this book is very well illustrated. It gives clear instructions on how to dress the patterns as well as advice on how to fish them.

Fly Tying by Sugg, Whitehead and Vare, published by Rod and Gun Ltd. An excellent book giving complete photographic sequences in the various stages of fly dressing.

SPECIALIZED SUBJECTS

Fishing the Dry Fly by Dermot Wilson, published by A. & C. Black: Again primarily for the river fisherman, but there is some thoroughly sound advice on dry fly presentation, which can be put to good use during reservoir fishing. Appendix A of this book includes a most valuable summary on all questions of tackle and Appendix B contains some excellent drawings of knots suitable for nylon whether in use for river or reservoir fishing. Appendix C contains a number of recipes for cooking the end product.

Nymphs and the Trout by Frank Sawyer, published by A. & C. Black: The author has put on record all that he has discovered during a life-time of fishing experience on this specialized aspect of fly fishing.

Pursuit of Stillwater Trout by Brian Clarke, published by A. & C. Black Ltd. An exceptionally well written book about one man's frustration at catching little or nothing by the chuck and chance method and what he did in order to achieve success. Excellent colour plates are included of the principal insects of importance to the reservoir trout and the fisherman.

Fishing for Lake Trout by Conrad Voss Bark, published by Witherby. The author gives advice in clear terms upon the success which can be achieved by fishing very few patterns and this book will be of special interest to the reservoir fisherman who wants to succeed with nymph tactics.

BOOKLETS

To Cast A Trout Fly. This excellent booklet was prepared by Messrs Farlow and Hardy Brothers in conjunction with Scientific Anglers Inc. of America. It is a step by step guide to the different casting systems and is very well illustrated. The casting methods include the single and double haul styles, the side cast and roll cast. Detailed advice is included on the use of shooting heads for long-distance work.

The Truth about Tackle by Dermot Wilson, available from his business address at Nether Wallop Mill, Stockbridge, Hants: This booklet provides a most comprehensive description of every item of fishing tackle and gives sound advice on what to look for when selecting tackle for river or reservoir trout fishing. Every beginner must get a copy of this publication because it will help him or her to buy the right kind of tackle for reservoir trout fishing and will save wasted expense on unsuitable items.

Appendix C

Associations we should support

Trout, salmon and coarse fish must have clean water for survival. If pollution takes control the fish die and our opportunities for all kinds of fishing come to an end.

Organizations are in being to combat water pollution and safeguard our fishing. They depend upon voluntary subscriptions for financing their invaluable activities.

Towards the beginning of each fishing season, when you write off for your permit, you should take that time as a reminder to send whatever subscription you choose to either The Anglers' Co-operative Association at Westgate, Grantham, Lincs., or The Salmon and Trout Association, Fishmongers' Hall, London E.C.4. If you write to the secretary of either organization asking for details of its activities and location of regional branches you will find some very good reasons for lending your support.

Epilogue

I should like to end this book with a prayer. I do not know who wrote it but I think it is most appropriate for all of us who enjoy fishing of every kind in the peace and quiet of our treasured countryside.

God grant that I may fish
Until my dying day,
And when it comes to my last cast
I then most humbly pray,
When in the Lord's safe landing net
And peacefully asleep,
That in His mercy I may be judged
As good enough to keep.

Index